presented to

_____

by

_____

❦

Reawaken my soul by the grace of Your love,

*since it is Your commandment that
we love You with all our heart and strength*

*—and no one can fulfill that commandment
without Your help.*

—St. John of Alverna

Beside a quiet stream
Words of Hope for Weary Hearts

PENELOPE J. STOKES

J. COUNTRYMAN

Published by J. Countryman,
a division of Thomas Nelson, Inc.,
Nashville, Tennessee 37214.

Project Editor—Terri Gibbs

Designed by
The Eleazar Group
Nashville, Tennessee 37204

ISBN: 08499-5466-5

Printed and bound in Belgium

contents

foreword

*C*hristians today live in a frantic, troubled world. And, perhaps without realizing it, we have become a frantic, troubled people. We have bought into the American work ethic and applied it to our spiritual lives with a zeal that would make us the envy of a Fortune 500 CEO. We get a lot done, but—perhaps without even realizing it—we have become slaves to the *doing*, and have neglected the *being*. It's no wonder many Christians suffer from Chronic Spiritual Fatigue Syndrome.

"Come unto me," Jesus says to us, "and I will give you rest."

But more often than not, we respond, "Thanks for the offer, Lord, but there's just too much to do."

We don't consciously choose to be frazzled folks. We don't want to be rushed and harried, overworked and over-booked. We don't want to live in a maelstrom of chaos, sucked under by a riptide of responsibility. Most of us, if we took time to think about it, would rather live in peace and tranquility. We'd like our lives to demonstrate something different, something better, to those around us. We'd prefer that our relationships be indelibly marked by the grace of God.

But we can't get grace on the go, ordering up a bucket of peace with a side of serenity at the Holy Spirit's drive-in. If we want to find restoration for our weary souls, we need to immerse ourselves in the nearness of God's presence. We need to give ourselves permission to take a long soak in the healing waters of the Spirit.

There is a way out, a way to break free from the bondage of weariness, the compulsion to perform. Escape lies in a spiritual principle we often overlook. "My yoke is easy," Jesus said. "My burden is light."

An easy yoke? A lighter load? Are we dreaming? Is it possible? More importantly, is it *spiritual*?

Come. Let's journey together into the depths of God's grace, into healing waters of mercy and love. Let's sit down beside a quiet stream—and listen.

Let's find out.

part one

Shallow Brooks and Silent Grottos

Take from our souls the strain and stress
And let our ordered lives confess
The beauty of thy peace.

—John Greenleaf Whittier

the super-saint syndrome

Perhaps you've met her—Super-Martha,
the woman who says "yes" to everything.

She spends her days driving kids to school, to piano lessons, to church youth rallies. By night she makes vegetable costumes so nineteen first-graders can represent stalks of asparagus in a twelve-minute drama about the Four Food Groups. On Monday she bakes fresh brownies, because on Tuesday morning she hosts a women's circle in her home...and she wouldn't be caught dead serving grocery-store cookies.

Sunday, the Sabbath of rest, is Super-Martha's most hectic day. She arrives at church at seven-thirty, oversees the nursery during the early worship service, teaches Sunday School, then plays the piano for the senior choir. After service, she dashes down the back stairs to the fellowship hall to arrange tables for the potluck dinner. A little before three, when the fellowship hall has emptied out, she washes dishes, puts everything away, and sets up for the Monday morning men's breakfast. By four she arrives home—her husband and kids have been there for hours—to find the living room littered with Sunday papers, the television blaring, and the dog begging to go out.

The telephone rings. It's Mabel Jefferson, asking her to coordinate the church's clothing and food drive. "You're so good at that kind of thing; nobody else can do it as well."

Super-Martha says "yes," of course. It doesn't even occur to her to say "no." Christians are supposed to be unselfish.

Aren't we?

Well, yes and no. When the original Martha, in the Bible, launched into her super-saint mode and criticized her sister, Mary, for sitting around doing nothing but listening to Jesus, the Lord gave her—and us—a surprising commentary on priorities. "There is need of only one thing. Mary has chosen the better part, which will not be taken away from her" (Luke 10:42).

There's nothing innately wrong with *doing*, of course. The dishes pile up; the laundry doesn't wash and dry itself; the kids and the dog need to be fed.

But we don't take enough time to sit quietly at Jesus' feet. We rush and hurry and run ourselves ragged. We keep on going, even when our bodies and souls scream out for us to stop. No wonder we're tired, drained, utterly exhausted in body and in spirit.

Only one thing is needed. Time with God. A place of settling, where our souls can be nurtured and encouraged to grow.

Becoming is important, too.

the weary self

*L*et's admit it.

We're exhausted people. Super-Martha isn't the only one who falls prey to the compulsion to keep on doing. We run ourselves into the ground, and it's not just our bodies that suffer. We've also lost our *selves* along the way.

In recent years, *self* has become a disreputable word among religious types. It's understandable. With the rise of popular psychology, individuals have become more aware than ever of the importance of "taking care of themselves," of understanding their inner motivations and struggles.

But coupled with an individualistic society that encourages us to "look out for Number One," such psychological insight sometimes results in a pendulum swing toward self-absorption. Many of us have spent years trying to please everyone but ourselves. When we realize the futility of such a quest, the result can be a knee-jerk reaction in the opposite direction—the determination to please *only* ourselves. When we finally learn to say "no," we say it all the time—sometimes loudly, and with great emphasis.

But eventually, we settle into a more natural rhythm. We achieve a sense of balance. Instead of always saying "yes"—or "no"—we say what is appropriate to the situation...and to the condition of our schedules and our souls.

The problem is, balance in the Christian life can be hard to come by.

Usually we fall prey to one of two extremes. Either we put ourselves first and slip into spiritual pride, or we put others first and plunge into self-imposed martyrdom. And both extremes can be subtle self-deceptions under the guise of "putting God first."

When Jesus was asked, "Which is the greatest commandment?" he replied, "'You shall love the Lord your God with all your heart, and with all your soul, and with all your mind.' This is the greatest and first commandment. And a second is like it: 'You shall love your neighbor as yourself.' On these two commandments hang all the law and the prophets" (Matt. 22:37–40).

Not "love your neighbor the way you love God." Love your neighbor *as yourself.*

How do we love others? By extending grace...compassion...understanding... care. We cut them a little slack when they mess up. We forgive them. We affirm them in their attempts to seek God. We encourage them to keep on trying, even when they've failed. We offer hope, and solace, and comfort.

Dare we do less for ourselves?

It's true, Jesus didn't directly command us to "love ourselves." But inherent in the second of the "greatest commandments" is the implication that we as human beings *do* love ourselves, and that as an extension of our love for God and ourselves, we are called to love and care for others.

Yet sometimes we mistakenly assume that our "love for God" must always be demonstrated in sacrificial service to the church. We interpret "loving others" as denying our own needs and being enslaved to the expectations of those around us. We even teach our children to sing, "J–O–Y...Jesus, then others, then you...what a wonderful way to spell J–O–Y."

Not always. Sometimes putting yourself last spells frustration... depression...fatigue.

But we're desperately afraid of being perceived as selfish. So, like Super-Martha, we work hard, trying to prove our selflessness, trying to demonstrate our commitment to God.

But our *work* doesn't always result in joy. We get worn out and resentful.

We make a grave mistake when we assume that what we *do* can substitute for who we *are*. Sometimes our Christian activity is less a reflection of love for God than love for the praise of others.

We need to remind ourselves from time to time that we are loved just as we are. Christ, who died for us when we had done nothing to deserve such a sacrifice, lives within us according to the same standard.

If we don't take time and space for ourselves, to nurture our personal relationship with God, our "works of love" become "dead works," motivated by fear or the need for performance rather than by love for God or for our neighbor.

Someone needs to tell Super-Martha the truth: It's not a sin to care for your own soul.

It's a spiritual prerequisite for a deep relationship with God.

sacrifice and burned-out offerings

In 1920, Edna St. Vincent Millay
wrote a poem that accurately
describes many of us:

My candle burns at both ends:
It will not last the night.
But ah, my foes, and oh, my friends—
It gives a lovely light.

It reminds me of that old hymn, "Let Me Burn Out for Thee," which we often take as a personal challenge. We believe that by exhausting ourselves in the service of God, we will somehow become nobler, more spiritual.

Perhaps we need to ask ourselves a hard question: Has God called us to "burn the candle at both ends," or is it burning due to motives that may be hidden even to ourselves?

In the Sermon on the Mount, Jesus gives us a clue to the secret incentives that may drive us. When you give alms, pray, and fast, Jesus instructs, do it privately. Don't sound the trumpet and call attention to your good works. Those who are praised by others, Jesus says, "have already received their reward" (Matt. 6:2).

The Lord doesn't ask us to exhaust ourselves, to run ourselves ragged in outward service and work. God doesn't demand that we drain our inner resources, that we deplete ourselves—heart, mind, and soul—in an effort to become more spiritual. Jesus offers rest, a lighter yoke, an easier burden than the one we impose upon ourselves. God offers grace and mercy, not a schedule so full we come to resent the Lord we claim to love and serve.

Of course we're called to fast, to pray, to give alms—both our money and our time and abilities—as a response to the love and grace that has been extended to us. But the sacrifice we need to draw us into relationship with God has already been accomplished. The era of burnt offerings is past. The time of grace is upon us.

We don't need to burn the candle at both ends.

the

sabbath

of the

soul

We hear others say it now and then. Perhaps, we've even uttered the words ourselves: "I need a little time for myself."

An un-Christian sentiment? A self-centered mindset?

Perhaps not.

The Bible gives numerous examples of people who took time for their own souls. Jesus himself often "withdrew to lonely places" (Luke 5:16), and on one occasion, when he was asleep in the boat, the disciples awoke him in middle of a storm. "Don't you care if we drown?" they asked (Mark 4:38). Jesus was taking time to rest, preparing himself physically, emotionally, and spiritually, for the ministry before him. His disciples thought he was being selfish.

The Lord, however, has a different word for it. God calls it *Sabbath*.

On the seventh day, God rested from the labors of creation, and commanded that we follow that example. "Six days you shall labor and do all your work. But the seventh day is a Sabbath to the LORD your God; you shall not do any work....Therefore the LORD blessed the sabbath day and consecrated it" (Exod. 20:9-11).

Why did God give us a Sabbath? Because we need rest. Not just physical rest but soul-rest, the chance to regenerate our spiritual power cells and renew communion with the Almighty.

It's up to us, in our everyday choices and personal priorities, whether we will become shallow brooks or silent grottos. We can be noisy, busy Christians splashing over obstacles below the surface as we hurry on to the next item on our schedule...or we can be placid, deep pools of serenity—tranquil waters of peace in a harried, fractured world.

If we want to become deep pools, mighty reservoirs of spiritual life, we need to incorporate the Sabbath into our daily lives. That means not just taking off one day out of seven, but perhaps spending one hour out of seven in quietness and contemplation; one minute out of seven in silence and reflection.

The Lord gave us the Sabbath for a reason.

We need peace and quiet...a little stillness amid the turmoil.

We need intimacy with God— we need the Sabbath of our souls.

who am I, anyway?

I entered college during the turbulent sixties. My friends and I wore fringed leather jackets and floppy hats. We strummed guitars and sang protest songs, picketed for civil rights and the end of the Vietnam War.

We were the Lost Generation, middle-class pseudo-hippies who underwent the most bizarre metamorphosis in history to emerge as the materialistic Baby Boomers of the nineties.

Back then, we were trying desperately to "find ourselves." We talked a lot about being real, about taking off masks, about showing what was truly inside. I'm not sure we knew quite what we were asking.

But one of my friends knew. One morning I came into the dormitory bathroom and found her standing in front of the mirror, staring. Just staring.

"Sometimes I look at myself," she finally said with a haunted expression in her voice, "and I wonder what's inside. I have this feeling that if I take off all my masks, *there won't be anyone underneath.*"

A chill went through me. She realized something the rest of us hadn't so much as considered: it can be a terrible shock to face the reality of what's inside.

Perhaps that's why so many of us run from the reality of self-awareness, immersing ourselves in work and frantic play. We don't want to look inside. We don't want to see what we really are—or aren't.

Perhaps we're afraid of our need for grace.

For many of us, *need* is a nasty four-letter word. We don't want to need anything. Need means weakness, lack of self-sufficiency. Need means that when I look inside and face reality, I see a person who isn't quite what I want her to be. Need means I can't do it myself.

Exactly. Welcome to the world of authentic Christianity.

The foundation of our faith, after all, is our undeniable need for the grace of God in Jesus Christ. Paul said that our righteousness is "through faith for faith," (Rom. 1:17) and that faith itself is a gift of grace (Eph. 2:8–9). If we truly want to live by grace in our outward lives, the process has to begin from within. The hidden, healing stream of grace must be discovered and allowed to flow in our innermost souls.

We must take the time to know ourselves, to develop our individual relationship with God. To be at peace with who we are, and who we are yet to become.

know thyself

S ocrates said it; Pope repeated it; philosophers and poets in every generation have returned to the truth of the maxim, "Know thyself." For the Christian, self-knowledge is essential—first to salvation, then to the ongoing, ever-changing relationship with God.

Initially, we must acknowledge our need in order to come to the Savior. And then, I think, we ought to pray for an honest, realistic view of our own capabilities—both in Christ and apart from God. For when we become aware of our capacity for both good and evil, we will be drawn continually to dependence upon the grace of God.

But spiritual awareness can be a pretty scary prospect.

In Psalm 139, David gives us a glimpse into the process: "O Lord, you have searched me and known me...you discern my thoughts... you are acquainted with all my ways...search me, O God, and know my heart; test me and know my thoughts..."

The implication is clear: Only God can truly know our hearts, and thus only God can reveal our innermost selves to us.

When we stop trying to fill our lives with meaningless activity and turn inward for a moment, we discover something wonderful: By God's grace, we are who we are. By God's grace, we will become who we were meant to be.

That doesn't mean we can just sit on our hands and wait for the Holy Spirit to reveal the truth to us like the unfolding plot of a made-for-TV movie. It does mean that whatever we discover about ourselves—whatever our gifts or shortcomings, whatever our fears or desires—God already knows all about us.

There's a great liberty that comes with knowing ourselves. A freedom that enables us to take risks, to grow, to change, to set sail for horizons we've only seen in our dreams.

Who are we? We are people, made—lovingly, and with great care—in the image of our Creator. We don't have to work ourselves into a frenzy to prove ourselves. We don't have to be super-spiritual or indispensable.

We only have to be who we are.

spa spirituality

For more than ten years I have grappled with a disease known as fibromyalgia—a chronic inflammation of joints and connecting tissues. Similar to arthritis, it results in pain and stiffness, fatigue and sleeplessness. A few years ago when I moved to the mountains, the house I bought came with a hot tub on the back deck. I had never owned a spa, having always considered it a frivolous luxury. But I soon discovered that even with an ancient model like the one I inherited, half an hour under the pulsating jets made a remarkable difference in my physical condition. I had less pain, more energy, more flexibility. Thirty minutes of hot tub time in the morning gave me hours more stamina at my work. Thirty minutes in the evening resulted in hours more uninterrupted sleep.

Recently, I moved again—this time to a house without a hot tub. And as soon as the boxes were unpacked and the furniture was in place, there I was, in the spa store, picking out a model called Shangri-La, in mystic emerald, with twenty-nine jets and a massaging lounger.

An unnecessary luxury? Some people might say so. But for me it is an investment in my physical well-being, in my ability to work.

And just as my body needs the pulsing waters of the hot tub to be able to function adequately, so my soul needs to be immersed in the waters of God's grace.

It's not enough to splash a little prayer on in the morning or to run through a sprinkling of God's mercy now and then. It's not enough to dabble our spirits in an hour of worship on Sunday or to dash into a drizzle of teaching every month or so. Our souls need to soak in God's presence.

It's no luxury, this time we spend in the healing waters of God's grace. It's neither excess nor indulgence to immerse ourselves in communion with our Creator. It's a spiritual necessity if we want to become the people God has created us to be.

Whose idea was it, after all, to lead us beside still waters and restore our souls? Wasn't it Christ who said, "The water that I will give will become in them a spring of water gushing up to eternal life" (John 4:14)?

Lean back. Relax. Soak in the waters of grace. Absorb God's love and acceptance.

Once you get used to it, you'll never settle for anything less.

*I*n Jesus' day, the Pharisees were the resident experts on prayer and fasting, on doing good and giving alms. In a manner of speaking, they were the workshop leaders who taught others: How to Do Quiet Time, How to Keep a Prayer Journal,...How to Be a Spiritual Giant.

Pharisees—both those of Jesus' day and their twentieth-century counterparts—attempt to establish a checklist of spirituality based upon their own practices. They know the "right way" to add up points for the merit-badge program— and they insist that their standards and systems apply to everyone else.

*a place of
quiet waters*

Jesus, however, brings us good news: We are dependent upon the grace of God, not our own power, to change our hearts and conform us to the image of Christ. The outward life of faith is rooted in inner grace, and the transformation from shallow pool to silent grotto can only be accomplished through a work of the Spirit.

To all who want to abandon the scorecards, give up the merit system, and enter into a place of deep quiet waters, Christ issues the invitation: "Come to me, all you that are weary and are carrying heavy burdens, and I will give you rest. Take my yoke upon you...and you will find rest for your souls. For my yoke is easy and my burden is light" (Matt. 11:28–30).

God extends to us, in our times of quietness, the opportunity simply to be in the Divine Presence...to sit at the feet of the Lord and listen, to allow the Spirit to work within us the changes that need to be wrought. It's an invitation of grace.

Grace does not demand performance. It does not weigh us down with expectations or frazzle us with activity. Grace accepts. Grace loves. Grace waits.

When we still our shallow, babbling hearts in the presence of Almighty God, we discover a deep and enduring peace, a silent strength that enables us not to *do*, but to *become*...not to prove ourselves, but to rest in the acceptance of what has already been accomplished on our behalf.

And then, in the quietness of our souls, we hear the whispered invitation, the blessed word: *Come. Come to me.*

Come...and I will give you rest.

like a river glorious

*P*eace.

The very word brings a stillness to the soul, a calm to the heart and mind.

We sing about peace: "When peace, like a river, attendeth my way...I've got peace like a river... Like a river glorious is God's perfect peace."

We gravitate to scriptural assurances about peace: "Peace I leave with you; my peace I give to you," Jesus says. "Do not let your hearts be troubled, and do not let them be afraid" (John 14:27). We want that inner peace. We're drawn to it. We may even pray for it. But do we understand what peace really is?

I'm not what you'd ordinarily call a peaceful person. I'm a woman of strong opinions, high passions, and great drive. For a long time I thought of peace as a kind of mind-numbing euphoria, rather like being on massive doses of pain-killers. Yet over the years I've discovered that peace is not a state of passivity, but a living, active work of God.

The hymns are right. Peace *is* like a river—moving, turning, plunging forward, carrying us downstream. It's not a static resting place, but an attitude of heart and mind that enables us to relax and let the current bear us up.

Sometimes we don't want to go with the flow. We get comfortable where we are. We'd prefer to dig our heels into the riverbed and refuse to budge. But if we're to live in peace, we need to accept the movement of the stream. The only peace we'll ever find that does *not* involve change is the final "Rest in Peace" on our tombstone.

The good news is, God knows where the river's going. The Lord's control, not our own, enables us to accept what we can't see and be at peace with what we don't know.

It's a matter of trust. Of living out what we claim to believe—that our Lord, the "immortal, invisible, God only-wise," understands what is best for us and will lead us where we need to go.

When we trust, we can be at peace. We can quit worrying about what other people think or how we're perceived. We can stop fumbling with the maps and attempting to figure out a better, faster, more efficient way to get where we're going.

The river beckons. Let's give God the rudder and enjoy the ride.

part two

❧

Deep in the Flow

Like a river glorious is God's perfect peace,
Over all victorious in its bright increase.
Perfect, yet it floweth, fuller every day,
Perfect yet it groweth, deeper all the way.

—Frances Ridley Havergal

deep river

The Mississippi River.

Big Muddy.

The river of
my childhood.

As a young girl, and later as a woman,
I stood on the banks of the Mississippi,
a mile wide at the Memphis bridge,
watching in awe as the dark waters slid by on their
way to the Gulf at New Orleans.

And even as a child, one puzzling awareness
stood out in my mind: the river was almost
completely silent.

"That's because it's so deep," my father explained.
"Deep waters are quiet."

I had heard the old adage, "Still waters run deep,"
and to my childlike mind, this translated into, *People
who don't talk much often have a lot to say.*

Now Daddy was giving me a different slant on
the proverb: Deep waters run still.

I knew the truth of what my father told me.
I had been to the Smoky Mountains and sat beside
the shallow streams that cascaded down from the
heights. I could barely hear myself think, much less
hear anyone speak. The shallows tended to be frothy
and noisy—happy waters, sometimes, but not
necessarily calming.

I suppose, if we were pressed on the issue, most
of us would prefer to be perceived as deep waters,
wise in the ways of God, settled in spirit, consistent,
emanating peace.

We want to be transformed. We want to grow.
We want the inward state of our souls to conform
to the image of Christ, and our outward relationships
and attitudes to reflect a Christlike lifestyle.

But we're not always sure
how to get there.

Most of us, if we're honest
with ourselves and with God,
would have to confess to a
certain level of internal chaos, a
shallowness that betrays us and
locks us into self-centeredness
and discouragement. We're not
at all certain that we are capable
of navigating the rapids and
finding our way to spiritual rest.

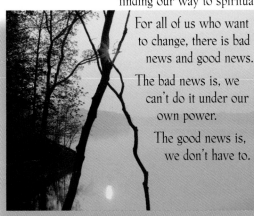

For all of us who want
to change, there is bad
news and good news.

The bad news is, we
can't do it under our
own power.

The good news is,
we don't have to.

The work of God in our lives
as Christians is exactly that—
the work of God.

We Christians claim to understand and live by grace. "By grace you have been saved through faith," we declare, quoting Ephesians 2:8–9. "And this is not your own doing; it is the gift of God—not the result of works, so that no one may boast."

But do we always believe it, or comprehend it?

We talk about our Christian faith as if the decision were ours alone, and we applaud ourselves for superior insight in recognizing our need for a Savior. We formulate plans for mission and ministry as if the responsibility for the faith of others rested solely upon our shoulders. We latch on to verses about manifesting gifts or developing the fruit of the Spirit as if we had the power to will those principles into effect in our lives.

Certainly, God calls us to minister to those around us. And without a doubt, God desires that the image of Christ be formed within us.

But the image of Christ is not a flashy, foaming whitewater of activity.

living by grace

We are not called to be always rushing downstream, trying to "get somewhere," to "do something for God."

We are called to *be*.

Consider Jesus' earthly ministry: He was born in a cow barn, with so little fanfare that only a handful of shepherds and a few star–gazing dreamers even knew about it. He spent the first thirty years of his life in obscurity, and most of his three years in public life was occupied not with preaching to the multitudes, but with touching the individual lives and

hearts of people
who lived on the
fringes of society.
When his followers
sought to exalt him into
prominence, he slipped through
the crowds and went off to spend
time alone with God.

Jesus knew the secret of becoming
the person God had called him to be:
private time in the deep waters of
God's presence.

If we want to live by grace—
not simply to accept grace for
salvation, but to *live* in grace in
every aspect of our live we need to
acknowledge our need for the hidden
work of God's nearness.

We need to go deeper.

We need to begin within.

As a child, I sang the song in Sunday school: "Deep and wide, deep and wide, there's a fountain flowing deep and wide..."

I knew about deep and wide. I had seen the mighty Mississippi.

Only years later, as an adult, did I have the opportunity to see the source of that deep, wide river. In Itasca State Park, in northern Minnesota, a small spring—narrow enough to step over—rises from the rock. The headwaters of the Big River.

But how? How does an insignificant spring become a 2000-mile-long waterway, carrying commerce and prosperity on its currents? How does a little trickle from Minnesota become the mighty Mississippi? How does it grow deep and wide?

By giving itself time and distance to carve out a course for itself. By joining with other streams along the way to multiply the power. By digging into clay

deep and wide

and bedrock, a little at a time, until it deepens and settles and quiets itself into a slow-moving, life-giving flow.

How do we grow deep and wide? The Lord who created and redeemed us will not impose spiritual depth upon us. We have a choice. We can rush headlong over the rocks, making noise and splash. Or we can rest in God's presence and develop a spirit of quietness and depth.

But we can't do both.

Most of us in the Christian community are caught up with being "wide"—spreading our spiritual and emotional energies far too thin, dabbling here and there and making a splash now and then. We haven't given ourselves the time or the opportunity to go deep.

A quart of water in a container has substance and depth. It can float an egg, cook pasta, quench a thirst. That same quart of water, poured onto patio stones, spreads out. It seems bigger, somehow, than a quart. But appearances can be deceiving—the wider it spreads, the shallower it becomes.

If we want to experience the deep waters of God's grace, we need to understand the importance of containment. We need to recognize that only God has an unlimited store of energy and creativity. The rest of us have limitations. We can pour out the waters of our spiritual resources and let them spread wide and shallow, or we can make a conscious decision to focus our energies on developing depth.

Still waters run deep.

Deep waters run still.

Be still. Go deep. Wait, and see the power of God spring up within you.

I'll be the first to admit it: I have real trouble finding the opportunity to be still. I have pressures and deadlines and work that has to be done *now*. I have responsibilities at home—friends and loved ones to care for, dishes to wash, beds to make, cars to get repaired. I rarely take vacations, and when I do, they usually end up being research trips, speaking engagements, or long-overdue visits with long-distance relatives.

I've heard about people who schedule a two-week vacation and then stay at home. Supposedly, they write letters, read books, enjoy a leisurely brunch at their favorite restaurant. They visit local attractions. They go to the movies in the middle of the day. They sit on the deck with their morning coffee and watch the sun rise.

It hasn't worked for me. If I take time off and stay at home, I end up *refinishing* the deck, not sitting on it. *Writing* books, not reading them. Exhausting myself doing all the

learning

to be still

postponed jobs that have needed doing for six months, not being still. When the vacation's over, I need another two weeks just to recover!

Most people, I suspect, are a lot like me when it comes to being quiet and resting in Christ's peace. We find ourselves rushed and harried with the demands of job, family, home, and church. We allow *doing* things for God to substitute for *being* with God.

If we truly desire to focus on our relationship with the Lord, to get off the running path and immerse ourselves in the deep waters of communion with the Almighty, we may need to be intentional about it. We may need to schedule a getaway with the Lord.

Go ahead and plan it. Write it on your calendar: *Lunch in the park with God.* Find a time and place to be still, to calm your soul in the presence of your Creator.

Whatever you left undone will be waiting for you when you get back.

For now, just take a moment with God...and rediscover peace.

the secret place of silence

A few years ago, I had an experience that became a turning point in my spiritual life. I made a retreat—three days of silence and solitude among nearly one hundred other seekers of God. There was no agenda, no teaching, no singing, no small group discussions. Just seventy-two hours of silence, including silence at mealtimes, broken only by an hour of corporate worship and communion every morning.

The first five hours or so was sheer torture. My brain swirled with a whirlwind of unexpressed thought. I couldn't pray, couldn't read, couldn't seem to settle down. But after a while, the silence seeped into my soul, and my mind and heart quieted into an attitude of reverence and anticipation.

And then God began to speak—not audibly, but deep in my spirit. Words of comfort and healing and direction. And more importantly, without words, a sense of the Divine Presence unlike anything I had ever known.

It was a holy time, a true holiday with the Lord. When the retreat ended and I went back into the "real" world, I felt overwhelmed by the noise, the rushing and chaos around me. I wanted to whisper to everyone: "Shhh. Be quiet. Listen."

Wilderness time is a holiday—a holy day set apart with God. It's an opportunity for strengthening, for restoration, for calling, for empowering.

And we don't need to live in the wilderness like full-time hermits, cut off from human society. We just need to go there from time to time, as Jesus did.

Your wilderness doesn't have to be a literal expanse of desert with miles of emptiness in all directions. You can find a solitary place in the kitchen after dinner, when everyone else has escaped to the living room. You can be alone with God in the bathtub, or on the porch, or in the back yard. You can find a place of quietness with God during your commute to work—with the radio turned off—or in your office with the door closed. You can lie on the floor in the nursery while the baby takes her nap. You can sit in the den with headphones on, listening to quieting music while the chaos of family life goes on around you.

Wherever you find your place of solitude, God can meet you there.

But find it, wherever it is...for it is life to your soul.

the hidden door

In C. S. Lewis's classic tale *The Lion, the Witch, and the Wardrobe*, the children—Peter, Susan, Edmund, and Lucy—enter through the door of a wardrobe and pass into a dense, snowbound forest, a wilderness of sorts. They don't know it quite yet, but they have entered Narnia—a magical land that ultimately becomes more real to them than their own world. In Narnia, they meet Aslan, the great Lion King, and in the process of relationship with him, discover their own inner capacities for good and evil. They grow and change, and ultimately come to rule the land in peace.

Our own solitary place with God can become a kind of "wardrobe door" for us, a portal that leads us into a new land of discovery—about God and ourselves. When we commit ourselves to times of solitude with the Lord, we cannot know what will happen...how we will change, in what directions we might grow. But we can be certain that time with God will result in something good, something beneficial for us and for those around us.

Sometimes our commitment to contemplation results in a conviction that God is calling us in new directions. When Moses entered into the wilderness, he met God face to face and heard the Voice of Jehovah in the Burning Bush. Ultimately, he was called—and prepared—to lead his people out of bondage.

At other times, quietness before God simply results in a deeper level of personal peace and spiritual intimacy. The Almighty doesn't command us, "Work hard; fill your schedule with activities, and you will see my face." Instead, our Lord whispers, "Be still, and know that I am God" (Ps. 46:10).

The problem is, we are not very adept at being quiet, at listening instead of talking. Our prayer times are often filled with requests but lacking in empty space, in silences that might, if we waited a little while, be filled with the presence and power of God.

Take a moment to listen.

Be still,

and you will

discover that

God is God.

vacation or holiday?

When Americans talk about taking time off from work, the word we most often use is *vacation*. The root: vacant. Empty. Void of activity.

The British, on the other hand, favor a different term: *holiday*. A holy day. A day set apart.

We may look at our crowded, overscheduled, stressed-out lives and say we need a vacation. But what we really need is a holiday, a holy day—a day apart with God.

In the lives of great men and women of faith, we discover an important principle about uninterrupted time with God. Moses met God in the desert, and there learned God's name and his own mission for freeing the Children of Israel from the bondage of Egypt. In the wilderness, God provided water from the rock (Exod. 3). Paul, after his conversion, spent three years in the wilderness in preparation for his ministry to the Gentiles (Gal. 1:17–18). Jesus himself, following his baptism, was "led by the Spirit into the wilderness" to face the Enemy's temptations and find strength for his calling as Messiah (Luke 4:1–14).

The promise of God is clear: "I give water in the wilderness, rivers in the desert, to give drink to my chosen people...that they might declare my praise" (Isa. 43:20–21).

It's a glorious thought, being present when God demonstrates such divine power. Water gushing forth in desert places. Water streaming from the rock.

There's only one catch: we have to be in the wilderness to participate in the miracle.

Moses and Paul and Jesus didn't wander into the wilderness by accident. God led them there, to a place of solitude where they could give the Lord their undivided attention.

Yet for most Christians, the wilderness raises unpleasant images of dryness, isolation, struggle, even death. We don't pray to be set down in the wilderness, and we rarely go there without resistance.

But only in the wilderness can we experience the miracle of water from the rock.

Only in the wilderness—in a place where the voices of distraction are silenced and the noisy shallow brooks are stilled—can we find the spiritual depth our souls long for.

Only in the wilderness can we truly experience a holiday with God.

sixty seconds of stillness

Once, in a church I attended, a young intern was serving as worship leader. When the time came in the service for silent reflection and confession, she invited the congregation to sit in quietness for a moment and allow God to speak in their hearts.

Then she waited. Completely at ease and composed, she stood before the altar as silence descended over the group.

Feet shuffled. Bulletins rattled. A few people coughed.

Still she waited, saying nothing.

A few eyes opened, and people began to shift uncomfortably in their seats.

She waited a little longer.

At last she went on with the pastoral prayer, and sighs of relief ascended from every corner of the sanctuary.

After the service I asked her how long the "silent prayer time" had gone on.

"I timed it," she said with a grin. "It was fifty-two seconds."

Less than a minute! Not even sixty seconds of silence in the presence of God, and an entire congregation grew antsy and restless.

Perhaps we're all a little uncomfortable with silence. Maybe that's why we fill our environments with meaningless, distracting sound—why we fill our "quiet" times with droning prayers and a multitude of words.

But just as emotional intimacy cannot be based on superficiality, so an intimate relationship with God cannot be based on spiritual small talk. Sooner or later we've got to "be still" if we are to "know that God is God."

And how do we learn to be still? By waiting through the disturbing, self-conscious moments until our hearts and minds grow comfortable with silence. It takes practice.

You don't need words to get through to God.

All you need is a mind attuned to the Lord's voice, a soul willing to wait.

Block out the distractions. Listen.

a life of devotion

Most of us, as Christians, have a pretty good idea of what "devotion to God" means. It means setting aside regular time for prayer and meditation, for Bible study. It means making a plan, having an agenda, putting it on our calendars—whatever we have to do to make sure we spend time with God.

But if we're not careful, we can turn valid spiritual disciplines into a frantic effort to "get it done"—to fill the necessary quota of prayer time, Bible reading, spiritual journaling, or a dozen other "necessary" activities for maturity. God does not want our meaningless rituals. God wants our hearts.

"What to me is the multitude of your sacrifices?" says the LORD; "I have had enough of burnt offerings" (Isa. 1:11).

Our intentions may be well-placed, but a lot of our frenzied religious activity falls into the category of burdensome "burnt offerings"—or in the case of the modern Christian, "burnt-out offerings." We scramble to rack up points with the Almighty as if our very souls depended upon the acquisition of celestial merit badges. "The one who dies with the most points wins."

And so we have become a weary people, a people desperately in need of grace.

We cannot become deep, silent pools when our riverbeds are filled with the boulders of self—imposed—or church—imposed—expectations. Yes, we do it to ourselves. But the religious system sometimes helps our legalism along, laying regulations and expectations and limitations upon us.

God, however, imposes no such artificial boundaries or regulations upon our spiritual intimacy with the Lord who loves us. There is a vast difference between having a prayer time and praying...between attending worship and worshiping.

God is more concerned with our life of devotion than with our devotional life.

We do not have to follow an approved format to come into the presence of the Lord, to find a place of deepening, and of peace. Our times of quietness, our moments of contem—plation with God, do not have to conform to some artificial standard or rule.

The important thing is that we have them.

face to face

In C. S. Lewis's mythical novel, *Till We Have Faces*, the central character, Princess Orual, provides a striking visual image of the necessity for us to come to God with an understanding of ourselves.

Angry with the gods, Orual veils her face for many years and never lets her countenance be seen. Finally, near the end of her life, the princess comes to a reconciliation of her anger. And she writes: "How can [the gods] meet us face to face till we have faces?"

We cannot meet God face to face till we have faces.

Till we know ourselves...

Till we take the time to discover who we really are...

Till we acknowledge our need for grace.

And then we realize that we aren't called to be Super-Christians after all. We aren't asked to do everything. We aren't responsible for meeting everyone's expectations. We aren't required to be perfect.

We're invited to come.

Come...into an understanding of your own soul, of your capacity for good and evil, of the fruitlessness of your frantic activity and performance. Come...into the place of authenticity, where you know yourself and are comfortable with who you are in God. Come...into the deep waters of the Lord's presence, where you will be healed and made whole, lifted up and transformed.

When your countenance is unveiled and your soul revealed, you can meet God face to face...and find peace in becoming the person you were created to be.

Your *self*...in God.

part three

❧

Downstream, Around the Bend

*Be still, my soul! Thy God doth undertake
To guide the future as He has the past.
Thy hope, thy confidence let nothing shake,
All now mysterious shall be bright at last.*

—Katharina von Schlegel

where

the

current

flows

Just down the block, walking distance from my house, the French Broad River wanders its way through the mountain countryside. One Sunday afternoon, a few people from our little church gathered at the riverbank for a baptism. We had found a quiet pool, waist-deep, out of the main current. It was a touching, happy ceremony. But something didn't seem right. The river was flowing...north?

I was born and raised in the relatively flat lands of the Deep South, and I knew—or thought I knew—that rivers flowed south...down, toward the ocean. Toward the Gulf of Mexico. Like the Big Muddy charting its course from Itasca to New Orleans.

But not in the mountain ranges of North Carolina. Here the rivers run south, north, east, west—however gravity pulls them out of the higher ranges. Sometimes they even seem to flow uphill. These are not straight-arrow streams pointing toward the ocean, but twisting, winding serpents of water, subject to powers beyond their natural tendencies. Eventually, of course, they do turn south and head for open seas, but not before they confuse and befuddle even the most competent navigator.

That northbound river reminded me of what it can be like to negotiate God's will.

Somehow, we always think we should know which way we're going. We get out the map and compass, read the directions, and think we know which direction God is leading us. We've got it charted, planned, and figured out. And then a force beyond our comprehension begins to change the rules.

North? This needle says we're going north! But we're supposed to be going south, aren't we? Wait—now we've shifted direction again.

Where are we going, anyway?

Who's in charge here?

We want to know. We want God to speak clearly and plainly, telling us our destination up front so that we can get on with the business of being obedient.

We're Christians, after all. We have the mind of Christ, or so the Bible tells us. We're supposed to be able to discern where God's leading us. And from there on, it's pretty simple. We take a ruler, draw a line between point A and point B, and bingo! We're on our way. Everyone knows, after all, that the shortest distance between two points is a straight line.

But not on God's river.

*L*et's admit it—we have a problem with directions. As Christians, we're trained to "seek God's will." We search the Scriptures, pray fervently, seek counsel from others, listen for a voice from above.

We expect God's will to be some kind of celestial career counseling, where we take a spiritual-gifts inventory, evaluate our possibilities, and begin moving along the "right" course for our lives. Then we get frustrated and resentful—sometimes outright angry—when the wind shifts or the river bends and we find ourselves going in a different direction.

But wait.

We're falling back into old patterns again.

We're looking at what we *do* rather than who we *are*. We're more concerned about where we're *going* than who we're *becoming*.

So, what exactly *does* Scripture say about God's will?

More to the point, perhaps, is what Scripture *doesn't* say about it. It exhorts us to follow God's will wholeheartedly, to pray "thy will be done," to delight in doing God's will.

mapping out the journey

But it doesn't tell us, "this is the one path to your spiritual destination." It gives us general principles to live by. It doesn't give us a detailed travel plan.

If we must have a verse—just one—to hang onto, a verse that says quite directly, "This is God's will for your life," here it is:

"Give thanks in all circumstances; for this is the will of God in Christ Jesus for you" (1 Thess. 5:18).

For those of us who live in fear of making a mistake—who want to be told where to go, what to do, who to marry, what church to attend, what job to take—the Bible isn't much help. But for those who long for the liberated, abundant life, the Scripture brings very good news.

The Lord's perceptions about the journey into God's will are a little different from our own. We are concerned about the *outcome*—covering the most distance in the least amount of time, and tying up at the right dock at the end. God is concerned about the *process*—letting the journey itself be the goal, what it can teach us...the character it can form within us.

It's not just a trip; it's an adventure.

When I traveled to the Cotswolds years ago, I got my first glimpse of an English hedge maze. It was a marvel of co-creation between nature and the gardener—a high box hedge, intricately designed with passageways, twists and turns, dead ends, and...finally... one way out—only one. There was one right way to go, and only someone perched high above could see which paths led to victory and which ones ended in frustration.

the ins and

Negotiating a maze is an entertaining game, but it's a debilitating way of life. And too often that's our image of God's will—a near-impossible labyrinth, the challenge to find the "one right direction." The Lord sees the right way, of course, but doesn't tell us. And so we search frantically, begging for direction, fearful that choosing the wrong way may endanger our spiritual lives—or even our eternal souls.

outs of God's will

The Bible I read, however, does not portray God as a cunning adversary, but as a loving Creator. The search for God's will is not a puzzle to be solved, but a life to be lived.

The familiar passage in Romans 8:28 tells us that "all things work together for good for those who love God, who are called according to his purpose." But let's not stop there. What is the purpose of God? Verse twenty-nine tells us: that we might be "conformed to the image of his Son."

The prime directive of the Christian life is not that we "find God's will and do it," but that we become like Jesus. Like Jesus—who went through life touching those who were in pain, healing the sick, speaking words of hope and liberty to those who lived in despair. Like Jesus—who kept his eyes fixed on the One who had sent him. Like Jesus—who sought, first and foremost, to please God.

It's a matter of the heart.

And if our hearts long for the fulfillment of God's purpose, we need not fear making some fatal mistake. The river will twist and turn, bringing us to new branches, decisions to be made, new directions to take. But we can make these changes fearlessly, with confidence that we will learn and grow from the journey.

And growth, after all, is God's will for us in Christ.

the bend

beyond

You can't watch television nowadays without seeing advertisements for free psychic readings. Gullible people—even well-known celebrities—tout the empowering benefits of a glimpse into the future. Unsure about this guy you're supposed to marry? Call our "real psychics" (not actors) and find out whether to book the caterer or dump the chump. What about that job interview? Your personal stellar consultant can tell you if a career change will spell success beyond your wildest dreams or unimaginable disaster.

All of us are tempted, from time to time, with the seduction of seeing what's around the next bend. But as Christians, we call on God rather than the Psychic Friends Network. We pray for direction, hoping to hear a voice from heaven, hoping to eliminate the uncertainty of living in the present without knowing what the future may hold.

The fact is, we can *never* know what tomorrow will bring. Divine wisdom has withheld that information from us...for our own good. If we did know what waited for us in the future, we'd try to change our destiny—or we'd be completely overwhelmed by what we saw. Instead of letting us know the future, God gives us something even better: The presence of One who is able to guide us.

"Trust in the LORD with all your heart," Proverbs 3:5–6 exhorts us, "and do not rely on your own insight. In all your ways acknowledge him, and he will make straight your paths."

Trust. That's the key to what lies before us. Not enlightenment, but trust.

Trust enables us to navigate the river without being frantic about what lies beyond the next bend. We put our faith in a God who understands the risks and the outcome. A God who is all-knowing, all-wise, and all-loving.

A beloved hymn reminds us of that truth:

Be still, my soul! Thy God doth undertake
To guide the future as he has the past.

Be still, my soul. No matter what lies around the bend, no matter what risks we must take, no matter what the outcome, the God who created us and loves us journeys with us.

We may not know the future, but we know the One who knows the future. We trust—and that is enough.

I've seen it numerous times, but I still laugh when I come to a stoplight and read that bumper sticker on the car in front of me: *God Is My Co-Pilot*. Oh, really? And you consider that a good idea? Besides, the way some of those people drive, you'd think God was lying down on the job, taking a nap in the backseat.

God is my co-pilot?

But don't we often act that way— as if God holds the position of honorary consultant in our lives? We go to the Lord for advice now and then, but we aren't obligated to accept it. We didn't just fall off the turnip truck, after all. We've had some experience at this business of living, and we've got a pretty good idea what is best for us. It's okay for the Lord to paddle in the front of the canoe, but we'll do the steering, thank you very much.

If God is my co-pilot, I might want to re-evaluate the chain of command.

It's just human nature: when we steer the boat, we tend to gravitate toward what's familiar. We don't take chances. We don't launch out into deep water. It's much more comfortable to keep to the shoreline, where the current's gentler and the risks are minimal.

When God is at the helm, things get a little more interesting. We find ourselves facing challenges we'd never dreamed of, opportunities that stretch our faith to the limit. Instead of a pleasant Sunday afternoon cruise, we're signed on for extended sea duty, headed for ports we've never even heard of.

It's a scary prospect, letting the Lord take over the pilot's position. We'd rather hang onto the wheel, keep up the facade of being in charge.

But we don't grow in faith unless we abandon the rudder to One who knows far better than we do where we're going and what we'll discover along the way.

And in the long run, it's much less hazardous to allow God to steer the ship. The Lord we serve is a competent commander, able to lead us on a quest that will change our lives forever.

So pry your fingers off the controls. Go stand at the rail and let the wind blow through your hair. A grand adventure awaits you.

It won't be what you've expected. It will be something far more exciting— perhaps even a little dangerous. It will set your heart racing and bring you to a depth of trust you could never imagine possible.

white water

I don't recall if my parents taught it to me, or if it was something I just picked up, the way children learn much of what is important in their lives. However I acquired the conviction, I've been blessed. For I came to believe, at a very young age, that the future was an exciting adventure, filled with limitless opportunities. Like Alice stepping through the looking-glass into a world completely unknown, I eagerly awaited the revelation of wonders yet unseen.

My friend Jackie, on the other hand, grew up with a different view of the unknown. To her, the future represented a never-ending series of threats, a shadowed world fraught with unanticipated dangers. It took her a long time—and an abundant measure of God's grace—to overcome the fear of what tomorrow might hold.

Since none of us can know what waits around the next bend, how we face the future is a matter of attitude—whether we see it as welcome surprise or looming disaster. Inevitably, life brings us difficult times—storms, rough water, white-water rapids. Even the disciples, who had Jesus with them on a daily basis, encountered such difficulties.

They were out on the lake in their small fishing boat when a storm kicked up—a raging tempest that threatened to swamp the craft and drown them all. The wind was against them, and they couldn't get back to land. So where was Jesus when they needed help? Up in the mountains praying. And then, in the darkness of night—about the time the disciples had decided there was no hope at all—Jesus came, walking to them on the water. "Take heart!" Jesus says. "It is I; do not be afraid" (Matt. 14:22–27).

Don't be afraid. Jesus spoke those words *before* he reached the boat... *before* the winds died down...while the disciples still feared for their lives. *Don't be afraid.*

We need to remember those words when we round the bend and see terrifying rapids ahead, when storms crash around us and darkness closes in and the Lord is nowhere to be found. *Don't be afraid*. Even when God seems far away, even when you can't hear the whisper of comfort over the roaring of the waves, don't be afraid.

The storm is part of the journey, too. It can be an adventure rather than a threat, an exhilarating experience of the presence of God. For Jesus still walks on the surface of the storm, still calms the tempest around us— or the one that rages in our hearts.

Jesus is there...in the darkness...in the storm.

Your future is in good hands. Don't be afraid.

taking in the scenery

Several years ago, a friend and I took a week-long vacation at her parents' cabin on the Canadian border. The cabin overlooked a quiet bay in the Lake of the Woods, and one afternoon we loaded the boat with our fishing equipment and set out to explore the enormous lake with its thousands of islands.

It was a beautiful day. We didn't catch any fish, but we saw egrets in the shallows and a black bear watching us from the shoreline. Around sunset we started home, and then I began to panic. Every island, every inlet, every channel looked alike to me. From the position of the sun I knew what direction we were headed, but I hadn't the faintest idea how to get back to the cabin.

It's easy to get lost among the 710,000 islands of Lake of the Woods. I kept pointing, questioning, trying to help: "Shouldn't we be going this way? I don't remember that island. Are you sure you know the way?"

My friend, a bastion of patience, just smiled and nodded and steered the little boat on. At last we came into the main channel, and in the distance I could see the bridge spanning the narrows near our cabin. I let out a sigh of relief. We had made it. But I had been oblivious to a beautiful sunset while I was obsessing about finding the way back.

In spiritual terms, most of us waste entirely too much time worrying about whether we'll bypass the next turn, whether we've gotten turned around. Anxious about finding the "one right direction," we miss out on a lot of what God wants to show us along the way.

The disciples had a similar problem. When Jesus began to talk to them about the future, they balked at the idea that he was going away. "You know the way to the place where I am going," Jesus assured them.

But Thomas—dear, doubting Thomas—protested. "Lord, we do not know where you are going. How can we know the way?"

And Jesus responded, "I am the way" (John 14:4–6).

Most of us, I think, worry too much. Like Thomas, we want to know: Where are we going? How will we know the way? How long will it take us to get there? Are we there yet?

We don't need a map. We don't need detailed directions, explicit instructions about what bearing to take and how far it is to the channel that leads us home. All we need is someone in the boat who knows where we're going. Someone who will smile patiently and steer us through the narrows to our destination.

So sit back. Relax. Take in the scenery. Enjoy the sunset.

Jesus has a hand firmly on the rudder and will guide you safely home.

the boat will float

In recent months not one but two television networks have produced movies about Noah and his enormous boat.

It's not exactly the *Titanic*. No one falls overboard and drowns. The boat doesn't sink in a grand display of special effects. It's simply a story of audacious obedience to God, who knows what the future holds.

Noah, the Bible tells us, was a righteous person in an unrighteous world. When the Lord gave him the command, he gathered materials and built the ark to specification, rounded up the animals and his family, and waited. And then it happened. "The fountains of the great deep burst forth, and the windows of the heavens were opened. The rain fell on the earth forty days and forty nights" (Gen. 7:11–12).

Noah had faith. He had no outward sign the flood was coming—not so much as a cloud in the sky. He didn't really understand what the future would bring, but he responded to God. He built the ark, and then entrusted his life and the lives of those he loved to the boat. He didn't steer, didn't create maps and charts for the journey, didn't try to figure out where they were going. He just watched while God shut the door and waited as the ark was born up on the waters and set down again on the mountain.

My dad taught me a similar lesson when I fished with him as a young girl. "Trust the boat," he told me. "If something happens and we capsize, the boat will float. Hang onto it—don't strike out on your own."

Our lives, even as Christians, are fraught with uncertainty. Storm clouds gather. The rains begin to fall. Lightning and thunder strike fear into our hearts and make us tremble at the looming possibilities. God doesn't reveal the future to us, doesn't tell us what is going to happen or how things will turn out. But the Lord does give us assurance that when the floods come, we will be born up and brought to a new place in our relationship with God.

Resist the temptation to strike out on your own. Have faith. Wait.

Sooner than you expect, the waters will subside.

the tension of the unknown

All of us live with uncertainty, but most of us don't like it very much.

Every day, we face the perpetual questions, the unknowns of life in the real world: Is my kid being tempted to take drugs or engage in irresponsible sex? What if the car breaks down on a dark road in the middle of the night? What if I get sick, or disabled? What if I get laid off?

We grope for answers, and find more questions. We evaluate our options, only to discover that we have to pick the best among a lot of good alternatives, or the least bad of any number of not-so-attractive choices. We want to do the right thing—for ourselves, for our loved ones, for our relationship with God—but sometimes "the right thing" isn't nearly as clear-cut as we'd like it to be.

Some of us find security in savings balances, stock purchase plans, and retirement accounts. But what if the market crashes, or the accountant embezzles the 401K funds? Some of us put our trust in relationships. But what if my spouse becomes interested in someone else, or my friends move away? Some of us bank on education, experience, and marketable skills. But what if I have to start over, to go back to college, to change careers in mid-life?

What if...what if...what if...?

The truth is, we can never escape the tension of the unknown. We may be faithful, responsible, intelligent adults, but we can neither know nor control what will happen tomorrow. We can never be sure, except in hindsight, where our decisions and directions will take us in the long run.

"Follow me," Jesus said to a lot of different people and received a lot of different responses. Some dropped what they were doing and followed him. Some said, "Okay, Lord, but first I need to say good-bye to my family. I need to take care of my elderly parents. I need to pick up my last paycheck. I need to leave a forwarding address."

If we intend to follow Christ, however, we need to realize that we can't always wrap things up neatly, tie up loose ends, have answers to all our questions. Being in relationship with God is a journey of faith. And faith, Hebrews 11:1 tells us, is "the conviction of things not seen."

Faith means stepping out onto the water when we don't understand what can possibly hold us up.

Faith means rounding the bend into a branch of the river we've never traveled before.

Faith means resting in the assurance that, although the future may be unknown to us, it's not in the least unfamiliar to the One who leads us. A future filled, not with answers, but with hope.

My mother had a unique perspective about situations that didn't go quite right. On family vacations, if we got lost and drove fifty miles on the wrong road, she would say, "Well, it's an adventure." If the charming lakeside cabin we had rented turned out to be a broken-down, spider-infested shack on the banks of a moss-covered lagoon, she'd say—after calling for reservations at the nearest motel, of course—"Well, it's an adventure."

As Christians, we might do well to adopt that attitude toward the lifetime journey we're taking with God. Circumstances don't always turn out, up close and personal, the way they looked on the brochure. Disappointments come, right along with the wonderful surprises. Difficulties catch us off guard. But we learn. We grow. We change. And when we look back, we can usually say that the situations that brought pain also brought new insight, deeper understanding, a closer relationship with God.

Attitude is everything. We can see life as a test to be endured, a dismal maze that keeps us going around in circles. Or we can look beyond the difficulties and see the adventure.

adventuring with God

Adventure is never without its danger—in part, that's what makes it exciting, exhilarating, challenging. We stretch ourselves, go beyond the limitations that we've always accepted, find out what we're made of. And whether we succeed or fail, we become something more than we thought we were in the first place.

The disciples discovered what it meant to adventure with Jesus. It wasn't all thrills and miracles—curing lepers, watching the blind regain their sight, the lame walk, and the deaf hear. Sometimes Jesus fed five thousand with a little boy's lunch; sometimes his disciples were so hungry they gleaned the fields along the way. The

crowds gathered around, sometimes listening, sometimes threatening their lives. The same people who shouted "Hosanna!" one day yelled "Crucify him!" the next. But even when the crucifixion had been accomplished and evil seemed to have won the day, the adventure wasn't over.

Because adventuring with God isn't about circumstances—it's about character. What happens *to* us doesn't matter nearly as much as what happens *in* us. The ups and downs of life, our personal crucifixions and resurrections, our victories and defeats, our stormy days and serene sunsets, all work in concert to make us into the people God has created us to be.

We don't always know where we're going, but we set our sails to the wind.

Journeying with God is an adventure that will last a lifetime—and beyond.

part four

Drinking from Deep Waters

O Love that will not let me go,
I rest my weary soul in Thee;
I give Thee back the life I owe
That in Thine ocean depths its flow
May richer, fuller be.

—George Matheson

trees by the riverside

*A*fter a spring of heavy rains and flooding, we've had a long summer of drought in the mountains. The city is under a ban: no washing cars or watering lawns. The grass is drying up as the sprinklers remain idle. Those of us with private wells watch our pump gauges and pray that the underground springs will hold out until it rains again.

We need water.

In spiritual terms, too, drought can be frustrating, even frightening. We've all experienced it—times when we pray, but our supplications seem to bounce off the ceiling. Times when the Scriptures remain silent, answers refuse to come, and the presence of God seems very far away.

We long for the rain, the refreshing of God's Spirit, the hope that's renewed with a sense of the Lord's nearness. We force ourselves to keep on praying. We fast and beg and storm the gates of heaven for some sign that the Lord has not abandoned us.

But what we really need to do is wait. Wait and trust.

For God, who created, redeemed, and loves us, hasn't forsaken us. This time of spiritual dryness will pass, just as winter passes into spring, just as drought eventually is relieved by the rainfall.

The prophet Jeremiah, who knew a lot about difficult times, gives us an image of what it means to put our trust in God:

"Blessed are those who trust in the LORD, whose trust is the LORD. They shall be like a tree planted by water, sending out its roots by the stream. It shall not fear when heat comes, and its leaves shall stay green; in the year of drought it is not anxious, and it does not cease to bear fruit" (Jer. 17:7–8).

Like a tree planted by water. Our nourishment doesn't have to come from above, in signs and wonders, in miracles. It can come from below, where our roots go deep into the silent springs of God's grace.

If we depend upon the rain, we are likely to become frustrated and disappointed, rootless, like a tumbleweed that dries up and blows away at the first breath of wind. But if we sink our roots into the subsoil of God's love, if we look not to circumstances but to the certainty of God's faithfulness, we can endure drought and still bear fruit.

Don't be afraid when the drought comes and the heat beats down. The river is always there, ready to provide what you need for life and godliness. Let your roots go deep.

In time, the rains will come again. But until they do, you will stand firm.

cycles and seasons

It's autumn in the mountains—bright blue-sky days with temperatures in the sixties; crisp, star-studded nights dropping into the forties. The Blue Ridge Parkway and most of the rural highways are crowded with leaf-lookers: tourists straining to find the brightest maple tree, the most magnificent panorama of color climbing down the mountainsides.

But this fall, they may go home disappointed. The dry summer has taken its toll on fall colors and fruit. The apples aren't quite so full and sweet as they were last year. Wildfires have blazed charred trails across the slopes. Withered leaves already litter the roadways, and the vibrant reds and oranges we brag about are few and far between. Things just don't look as good as they usually do this time of year.

But the old-timers aren't worried. Our trees are strong. The oaks and maples have deep roots. They'll come back next year. And so will the leaf-lookers, in their vans and RV's, making their annual journey to the mountains.

There's a spiritual lesson in the browning trees on the hillside. Sometimes, in our relationship with God, drought seems to take its toll. The fruit we bear is less than perfect. Our leaves—the evidence of the Lord's grace in our personal lives and in our relationships with others—seem withered and colorless. Winter comes too quickly, when we haven't even had a chance to enjoy the blessings of autumn's bounty.

But one bad season is no reason to give up. Here in the mountains, we don't go digging up the apple trees or burning the maples off the slopes just because the fall harvest of Granny Smiths and the flaming color hasn't lived up to our expectations. We wait. We trust. We're pretty philosophical about it all. Next year will be better.

Spiritual life, like physical life, has its cycles. Rain and sun, planting and harvest, dormancy and resurrection.

Has it been a bad year? Don't despair. Don't give up. The fruit will come "in its season." Withered leaves will sprout again. Spiritual prosperity will come once more.

water

from

the

rock

Up on Flat Top Mountain, where the gravel road winds its way to the summit, water gushes from the rock. Literally. Right at the road, so close it's a little frightening, a cataract plunges down from a huge rock embedded in the hillside. I never pass that rock without thinking of the miracle.

With Moses at the helm, God began to lead the Children of Israel out of the bondage of Egypt, on a trek toward the Promised Land. But there was one catch: to get to the land flowing with milk and honey, they had to pass through the wilderness. No milk there. No honey. Not even water.

Unhappy with the situation and forgetting the promise, the people grumbled against God and quarreled with Moses. "Why did you bring us out of Egypt, to kill us...with thirst?" (Exod. 17:3). So God sent Moses on up to Horeb, and told him: "Strike the rock, and water will come out of it, so that the people may drink" (Exod. 17:6). Moses obeyed, the water flowed out of the rock, and the people were satisfied—for a little while, at least. History tells us that even after the water, the manna, and the quails, they still complained.

Did the Children of Israel need water? Sure they did. Did God intend to provide for their thirst in the wilderness? Apparently so. But I wonder, just a little, what might have happened if they had trusted God's provision instead of griping and complaining about it. Perhaps they would have stumbled upon a different kind of miracle—an oasis, perhaps, or a well—something a little less obvious than water gushing from a stone in the desert. Would they, then, have asked the mocking question, "Is the LORD among us, or not?" (Exod. 17:7).

I wonder, too, about us modern Christians. In our private wildernesses, do we grumble and complain until we see water gushing from the rock, when the oasis is just over the hill? Do we find it hard to keep from griping when we don't see an immediate answer, when we're not given instant gratification of our spiritual or material needs?

The answer to the Israelites' question is a resounding YES. God *is* with us. God provides. We may get a spiritual spectacle—water from the rock, manna from heaven—or we may get a less flashy provision—an unexpected oasis, or a rich land that will yield its produce when we ourselves do the sowing and harvesting.

Either way, it's a touch of God. Either way, it's a miracle.

rivers in the desert

The desert, they say, has its own terrible beauty. I wouldn't know. I've always lived in green places. In the South, where lush rolling meadows caress the eye and tall pine trees grow skyward. In the Midwest, where early waves of wheat bow to the wind and bright crocuses push through the spring snow. In the mountains, where the soul is lifted heavenward on soaring blue-green peaks.

But I've seen photographs of the desert: arid waste places with not a sprig of growth in sight. I've witnessed time-lapse videos of the long-awaited rain when the dry ground soaks in the blessed moisture; the desert bursts into bloom as if by magic. It all happens so quickly, so unexpectedly.

Sometimes, in our spirits, it happens that way as well. "I will make a way in the wilderness and rivers in the desert," God promises, "for I give water in the wilderness, rivers in the desert, to give drink to my chosen people" (Isa. 43:19–20).

Some of us don't like being in the desert. When our spirits flag, our best efforts end in failure, and our relationships cause us no end of frustration, we don't really care what we can learn from the experience, or how close we might draw to God in our solitude. We just want to go home.

But whether we like the idea or not, all of us need to spend time in the empty spaces. The desert holds vast possibilities. It gets us back to basics. It gives us the opportunity to experience God in a new way. Out there, alone, we see things more clearly. The stars seem closer, and the heavens more accessible. And when the rains do come, the miracle of growth astounds us.

Feeling a little dry? A little isolated, there in your desert? Want to escape, to get back to your green places, and as quickly as possible?

Take a little time to look around. The days in the desert—or weeks, or months, or even years—are not punishment, but preparation. Take time to focus on the Lord, to get direction, to hear God speak.

To witness the miracle
of rivers in the desert,
you have to *be* in the desert.

quenching the inner thirst

new television movie is about to be released. I saw the trailers the other night—a suspense thriller about a town under siege. It's called *Thirst*. The waters have been poisoned, and amid scenes of panicked people running for their lives, a foreboding voice intones: *"It's 98 degrees outside. You can't drink the water. You can't swim in it. And you can't escape."*

Just the advertisement made me bolt to the kitchen to refill my iced tea.

Thirst scares us. We can live without food for weeks, but without water, we die in a matter of days.

How many of us, however, experience the same kind of immediacy in our thirst for God?

"As a deer longs for flowing streams, so my soul longs for you, O God," the Psalmist writes. "My soul thirsts for God, for the living God" (Ps. 42:1–2).

When we begin to go deep with God, we start to recognize our own need. Need for quiet times of peace and restoration in the presence of the Lord. Need to quench our thirst from the springs of living water.

But many of us don't take the time we need for refreshing. We keep going, keep doing, sweating it out for God. Our spirits get weak and shaky. We don't realize that we're depriving our souls of what they need to sustain spiritual life.

We can't survive long without water. We can't expect to take a sip or two one day a week and have our thirst quenched until the next Sunday rolls around. We need a constant infusion—every day, every hour—of the water that brings life to our souls.

When you're physically thirsty, your body tells you: your tongue swells, your mouth goes dry, and you can think of little else but getting a drink.

Spiritual thirst demands attention, too. When anxiety rules your heart, when frantic activity crowds your days, when the voices around you drown out the still small voice of God, it's time to stop and take in divine water.

Listen to your inner thirst. Take time to drink deeply of God's grace and mercy.

Your thirst will be quenched...but you will find yourself longing for more.

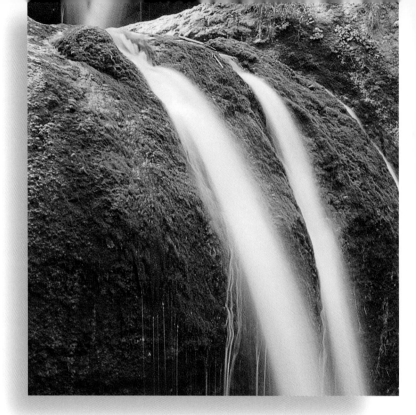

a watered garden

In my office, propped open on a bookshelf, stands a ragged old book, a beautifully-illustrated story that belonged to my mother when she was a little girl. In a childish cursive, her name is scrawled across the first page in thick black pencil, just above the title: *The Lovely Garden*.

It's the tale of Queen Yolande, wife of the vain, self-centered King Basil, who against her husband's wishes goes out among the poor and destitute of the kingdom to inquire after their needs. "What am I here for if it is not to make others happier?" she wonders.

And the queen does make others happier—so happy that a mysterious gardener creates for her a magic garden, where only the rarest fruits and flowers grow. The garden gate will open only for the pure of heart, and even King Basil cannot enter until he learns to live the password: "In my garden I plant seeds/ Of loving thoughts and kindly deeds."

We love gardens, don't we? Especially those of us who can't even make air fern grow. We love the serenity, the quiet wonder of living beauty all around us, the miracle of bud and blossom and fruit.

Our faith history begins in a garden—in Eden, that Paradise where our first mother and father walked with God in uninterrupted communion. Sin thrust them out of Paradise, and since that day, we have been trying to get back in. Back to the place of harmony with God, with others, and with all creation.

But God has something different in mind for us—not to go *back* to the garden, but to *become* the garden. "The LORD will guide you continually," Isaiah 58:11 reminds us, "and satisfy your needs in parched places...and you shall be like a watered garden, like a spring of water, whose waters never fail."

Imagine it—as we sink our roots deep into the Lord's love, by divine grace we can become, for ourselves and for those around us, a garden of wonder and spiritual nourishment. A place of tranquility and rest in the midst of a noisy, troubled world. A conservatory of serenity, where those beaten down by life can come to be healed and restored, empowered and cared for.

But to open the gate, we must live the password. We must give ourselves to God's purposes in our lives and let the Spirit create in us a place of healing, acceptance, and hope.

The gate stands open.

Come in. And bring others with you.

A few weeks ago, I passed through Nashville and spent an evening at the Opryland Hotel. I'd never been there, and I felt like a country girl come to the big city, craning my neck and exclaiming with wonder over everything I saw. Fountains danced with colored lights to the music of a grand piano. A five-story waterfall fed into a river that meandered for miles, it seemed, into a Delta town with a full-scale antebellum home perched on the levee and patio restaurants scattered along the shoreline—all indoors, all created by some architectural genius.

It was fascinating. It was awe-inspiring. It was downright unbelievable. But it wasn't real. Real rivers, you see, go somewhere—not just around the circle of a huge and complex system of hotel lobbies. Real rivers sustain life—fish and turtles and tadpoles and insects, and sometimes even an alligator or two. Real rivers move and change and take us places we hadn't anticipated going.

"How precious is your steadfast love, O God!" the Psalmist declares. "All people may take refuge in the shadow of your wings. They feast on

the river of delights

the abundance of your house, and you give them drink from the river of your delights. For with you is the fountain of life; in your light we see light" (Ps. 36:7–9).

The river that flows from the heart of God into our hearts isn't a big show put on to attract tourists. It's as real in spiritual terms as the mighty Mississippi. The river of God's presence offers us abundant life, food for the spirit, quenching of the soul's thirst.

Has your heart grown weary? Lie on the bank and listen to the murmuring of the waters as they rush by. Let the fresh breeze blow new energy into your being.

Does your soul feel grimy with the accumulated soot and smog of the world? Wash off in the shallows; dangle your feet in the current; feel the cool waters rush over you in a cleansing flood.

Are you thirsty? Drink deep. These waters will never run dry.

The river of God provides for our needs, but there's more. It's a river of *delights*—bright flowers along the banks, fish jumping in the rapids, sounds and sights and scents that bring us not merely *restoration*, but *rejuvenation*. Laughter. Joy. Renewal.

And a multitude of delights we haven't even begun to imagine.

the

spring

of

faithfulness

Faithfulness seems to be a scarce commodity in our world.

We make promises—to ourselves, to those we love, even to God—only to break them. Half of all marriages end in divorce. Single-parent families are the norm rather than the exception. Absent fathers have to be forced by the courts to pay child support. Friends betray one another. The ground at the foot of the corporate ladder is littered with broken bodies. To succeed, we have to swim with the sharks.

Or do we?

Judging from the amount of Scripture devoted to the subject, faithfulness is pretty important to God. But sometimes we misunderstand what it means. We think that to be faithful, we have to dredge up from within ourselves some kind of superhuman resolve, to hang on by our fingernails, to exert all our determination to be true to the promises we've made.

But faithfulness goes much deeper than what we *do*. It cuts at the heart of who we *are* in God, and what is happening in our spiritual lives. The Psalmist describes faithfulness not as effort, but as the inevitable outflowing of a soul right with God: "Steadfast love and faithfulness will meet; righteousness and peace will kiss each other. Faithfulness will spring up from the ground, and righteousness will look down from the sky" (Ps. 85:10–11).

Faithfulness will spring up...

A spring is a natural water source, bubbling to the surface of its own accord. To get water from a spring, you don't have to dig, sweat, strain, or work. You just have to hold out your hands and let the water flow.

Sure, relationships demand diligence. We have to work at them. We have to devote time and effort to nurturing them. But if we have given ourselves, heart and mind and soul, to the One who created us and redeemed us, faithfulness becomes a way of life, not a difficult task.

If we depend upon God's steadfast love in our lives, upon the righteousness that only comes from the Almighty, then faithfulness will flow from us like a spring of fresh water.

satisfaction

A few years ago they called it the "All You Can Eat Buffet." The very advertisement conjured up images of burly truck drivers sitting down at a table groaning with food and stuffing themselves for hours until they could barely stagger to the door.

Now we've gotten a bit more genteel. We've renamed the ritual "All You *Care* to Eat." The truck driver has been replaced with a sweet little grandmother protesting, "Oh, no thank you. I don't believe I care for more." Either way, it's a picture of complete gustatory satisfaction—or excess, depending upon your perspective.

In the sixties, the Rolling Stones sang, "*I can't get no satisfaction.*" They weren't singing about the buffet, of course, but the song became a byword for a generation. We're never satisfied. We're always looking toward the future—a higher paying job, a bigger house, more toys, more elaborate vacations. Sometimes, even, a younger and better-looking spouse.

But that's not the kind of satisfaction the Lord guarantees.

God's promise for prosperity and fulfillment isn't about what we own or what designer labels we wear or what kind of car we drive. Certainly, the Lord is concerned with our physical lives—food and shelter, clothing and love. But the all-you-can-eat buffet isn't high on the divine priority list.

Satisfaction in God has a different focus. "Hungry and thirsty, their soul fainted within them," the Psalmist tells us. "Then they cried to the LORD... and he delivered them from their distress...He satisfies the thirsty, and the hungry he fills with good things" (Ps. 107:5–9).

When we get discontented— reaching out for something more, longing for better things, restless for change—perhaps our *souls* are fainting within us, calling out to be delivered from our distress. We can charge the maximum on our credit cards, or we can turn to God, whose steadfast love feeds us in ways our dissatisfied world cannot understand.

Can't get no satisfaction?

Let God reach into your heart and satisfy your soul with good things. Spiritual things like joy and peace and direction; enduring things like love and hope and passion for life.

The Lord satisfies the thirsty and fills the hungry with an enduring contentment the world can never offer. Not even at an all-you-can-eat buffet.

joy from the well

We used to sing it in Sunday school—a rousing little song that never failed to evoke clapping and laughter:

> I've got the joy, joy, joy, joy
> down in my heart.
> Down in my heart.
> Down in my heart...
> Down in my heart to stay.

But I wondered as I grew older—*Why was the joy down in my heart to stay?* Shouldn't it be flowing out, spilling over to affect my life and the lives of those around me?

The prophet Isaiah thought so. "With joy you will draw water from the wells of salvation. And you will say in that day: Give thanks to the LORD, call on his name; make known his deeds among the nations; proclaim that his name is exalted" (Isa. 12:3–6).

I've heard people say that joy and happiness are not the same thing. I've said it myself, if I'm not mistaken: happiness is external, based on circumstances. Joy is like a deep current, unaffected by what's happening on the surface.

But don't we have that a little backward? Shouldn't the deep joy in our hearts have an effect on how we view our circumstances, how we deal with stormy weather and disappointment? Joy isn't something we cling to the way a drowning person clings to a life raft. Joy is the inner conviction that something is fundamentally right in our lives, in our relationships with God and others.

The well of salvation is deep and pure and clear. Drawing from it changes everything—not just our eternal destiny, but our daily lives. Salvation transforms our everlasting souls, to be sure, but it also alters our hearts and minds, our relationships, our attitudes and actions.

Let down your bucket into the well of salvation and draw up the water of life with joy. Shout out loud.

You've got the joy down in your heart—don't let it stay hidden there.

part five

Whirlpools and Riptides

When peace like a river attendeth my way,
When sorrows like sea billows roll—
Whatever my lot, Thou hast taught me to say:
"It is well, it is well with my soul."

—Horatio G. Spafford

sorrows like sea billows

After a much-needed night of steady rain, this morning dawned clear, cool, and sunny. A perfect autumn day. But as I went about the morning's errands—a trip to the polls to vote, quick stops at the post office and grocery store—the headlines from the newspaper stands brought me face to face with a less pleasant reality: the devastation wreaked by Hurricane Mitch. Houses and businesses destroyed, buried under water and mud. Families separated. Thousands dead and injured, even more homeless and destitute. Millions of dollars in damages.

We'd like to think that our lives as Christians would be free from such disaster. We hope and wish—even pray—for our little corner of the world to be placid, calm, untroubled. After all, didn't God promise us rest beside quiet streams?

But difficult times do come. Storms hit hard—not just physical ones that threaten our possessions, but emotional and spiritual ones as well. Relationships hit the rocks, faith is overwhelmed by the flood. Confusion besets us, and we're left with one of the huge unanswered questions of the universe: Where is God when the clouds roll in?

Job, that great biblical example of faith in the midst of despair, expresses for us all our feelings during stormy times: "Truly the thing that I fear comes upon me, and what I dread befalls me. I am not at ease, nor am I quiet; I have no rest, but trouble comes" (Job 3:25–26).

Many of us, however, have difficulty being as honest with God as Job was. Instead of understanding that rough waters are an inevitable part of our spiritual journey, we take the role of Job's "comforters." We question our own integrity. We confess imaginary sins. We figure that somehow we must be at fault when our lives seem to fall apart.

And certainly, sin sometimes does play a part in the difficulties we encounter. On occasion we bring trouble upon ourselves by the choices we make, and when that happens we need to turn back to our Savior. But we also need to understand that the whirlpools and riptides we encounter as we travel through life may simply be part of the process, the ways we learn and grow and strengthen our trust.

When the rough waters come, hang on tight. Don't be afraid to express your fears and questions. Job did, and in the end God spoke to him and revealed treasured truths about the Divine Nature that he couldn't have gained any other way.

Sorrows may roll over you like the billows of the sea... but as long as you hold onto God, you can say from the depths of faith: "It is well with my soul."

outrageous directions

*R*ecently a friend sent me a comic strip that made me laugh...and caused me to think. It shows a preacher, sitting on the hillside with one of his parishioners.

"So, Preacher," the parishioner asks, "what brought you to a dead-end town like Podunk Hollow?"

"God called me."

The parishioner thinks about this for a minute, and then responds, "Don't you have caller ID?"

I've felt like that preacher, on occasion. I've wished for caller ID, and wondered: What do you do when God's will doesn't make sense?

It's a question that troubles us all, from time to time. Logic seems to direct us one way; our best reasoning, our "pros and cons" list all point in the same direction. But something else—others call it instinct, a gut feeling; I call it the Spirit's leading—tells us *no*. Not that choice. Not now.

We're okay with the Spirit's leading as long as the outcome seems reasonable. But to step out in faith, without the finances or the spiritual resources or the emotional strength to do what we're being called to do? Then we balk, second-guess ourselves, and rationalize: "God couldn't possibly be directing me to do something so completely outrageous."

No? Consider the saints, the great ones of God. Abraham was told to leave his home and travel to a land he'd never seen.

Moses heard a voice from a burning bush instructing him to go back to Egypt to set the captives free. Noah was given plans to build a floating zoo. Mary, unwed, frightened, and little more than a child herself, received the announcement that she'd been chosen to bear the incarnate Immanuel.

When God seems to be leading us in outrageous directions, the experience can be a challenge to our faith—a whirlpool that sucks us into confusion and fear, a riptide that seems to pull the bottom out from under us. "I can't do that!" we protest. "I'm not equipped for the job."

That's what Moses said: "O, my LORD...I am slow of speech and slow of tongue...please send someone else" (Exod. 4:10, 13). But God did not allow Moses to be pulled under by the whirlpool of fear: "I will be with your mouth," God responded, "and [will] teach you what you are to speak" (Exod. 4:15).

Is God asking you to do something outrageous? To risk your comfort, or your security, or your reputation for the sake of obedience? Have faith, the faith of those who have gone before you into dangerous waters.

Faith is stronger than any riptide.

It's a favorite Sunday school story from childhood, a tale filled with drama and excitement. I can still see the flannel board pictures in my mind: Jonah, superimposed upon the midsection of the whale. On his knees, praying to be saved.

But Jonah didn't start out on his knees. He started out in rebellion.

In reality, it's a bleak story... a story filled with images of darkness, of separation from God. God gave Jonah the mission of bringing the truth—and perhaps repentance—to the wicked city of Nineveh. It could have been a great adventure, a wonderful opportunity to see the grace of God at work. But Jonah didn't like the call. The people of Nineveh didn't deserve the Lord's mercy, Jonah had decided, and being sent to them went against the grain of his own system of righteousness. Rather than responding in faith, he ran the other direction. It took being thrown overboard and swallowed by an enormous fish to bring him around to saying yes to God—and even then

in the belly of the whale

he did it reluctantly, with an attitude. With anger and bitterness (Jonah 1–2).

I've always been curious what the fish thought about his own encounter with God. For that, too, was an outrageous call: "Go, swallow my prophet, and hold onto him until he changes his mind." Whatever the fish's reaction, he, at least, was obedient. Who, I wonder, was the true prophet?

When life gets difficult, when God calls us to outrageous obedience, rebellion can be a whirlpool that drags us under. And no matter how much effort we put into redecorating the interior of that fish's belly, it's still a place of darkness. A place of separation from the One who has chosen and sent us.

One way or another, we end up on the shores of Nineveh. The question is, whether we go willingly or not.

We may not always understand why God works in such unconventional ways—why we need to be in a particular place at a particular time, or what the outcome of our obedience

will be. Even after the fact, we may scratch our heads in confusion and wonder, "What was *that* all about?" We may sacrifice a great deal to obey God, only to see no visible results from our efforts. The people of our Nineveh may not repent at all.

But the *outcome* is not the issue. Our *attitude* is what matters to the Lord. Our willingness to respond affirmatively when the Spirit nudges us, even when we don't know why.

Give the big fish a break. Start out on your knees.

Who knows what miracles of grace may be wrought when you say *yes* to God.

A new animated movie was released this spring—the story of Moses, *Prince of Egypt*. The bookstores are full of advertising periphery for the film: story books, coloring books, Moses dolls, tiny boats made of bulrushes. It hit the theaters with a bang.

floating amid the bulrushes

Yet the real tale of Moses begins not with a bang but with a whimper: a slave baby, marked for death, hidden by his mother until he was three months old and she could hide him no longer. Then the mother did something completely incomprehensible. She fashioned a basket, waterproofed it with pitch, and set the child adrift on the river (Exod. 2:1–4).

In modern times the woman's actions would be unthinkable—abandoning a helpless infant to the elements, leaving him to float into an uncertain future. We know, of course, what happened to the baby. It was all part of God's plan to set the Israelites free from Egyptian bondage. But his mother didn't know. She simply responded to the situation out of faith, and trusted God to take care of her son.

In our own journey of faith, we sometimes feel as if we are floating, too—caught in the whirlpool of cir-cumstance, unable to control our des-tination, subject to the currents and eddies of the river that bears us along.

We could take a lesson from Moses' mother. Control makes us comfortable, but it doesn't always get us where God wants us to go.

The Lord knew exactly where Moses was headed when he floated down the river in the bulrush basket. He was moving toward his future in God—first as an adopted Prince of Egypt, then as an exile from his own kind, and finally, after years of resistance, as the great Liberator who faced down the Pharaoh and demanded, "Let my people go."

We can never know, when we're floating out of control on the current, just where God is taking us. But we can trust. We can have faith. We can remember how the Lord has led us in the past, and be at peace.

Do you feel as if you're up the river without a paddle? Don't panic. The water is not your doom, but your salvation. The current will bring you to the place you need to be. And maybe, just maybe, it will be the first leg of a journey that will change your life forever.

dead ends and
new ways out

I spent last Saturday going around in circles in Atlanta.

I'm not familiar with the city, but I had a map and thought I knew where I was going. But I kept running into dead ends. *No Through Traffic*, one sign read. *No Outlet. No Return Ramp.* The signs might as well have said, *Just Forget It and Go Home.*

In our spiritual lives, too, we sometimes come to dead ends. We're so certain we've heard the voice of God and are following the Lord's direction. And then, without warning, a barrier. No more road. Not so much as a detour. Not even an alternate route.

That's the kind of dead end the Israelites came to when they followed Moses out of Egypt. Everything had looked so perfect. Moses had performed miracles not even the Pharaoh's magicians could reproduce. The Pharaoh had relented and let them go, millions of them, with all their livestock and possessions and even some of the treasures of Egypt. A new life awaited them in a land of milk and honey.

Or so they thought...until they looked up and saw a terrifying sight. The Red Sea stretched out before them, and behind them the Egyptian army was closing in.

There was no way out. They were going to die, all of them, right there on the banks of the sea. The only choice was to drown or be impaled on the point of an Egyptian spear.

And they did what most of us do when we come to a dead end. They lifted up their voices and howled. "Was it because there were no graves in Egypt that you have taken us away to die in the wilderness?" they screamed at Moses. "It would have been better for us to serve the Egyptians than to die in the wilderness" (Exod. 14:11–12).

What they didn't know was that there are no dead ends with God. No blank walls. No barriers that can't be overcome. "Do not be afraid," Moses commanded. "Stand firm and see the deliverance that the LORD will accomplish for you today" (Exod. 14:13).

We all know what happened at the Red Sea that day—a wildly dramatic miracle. The waters opened, the Israelites crossed over on dry ground, and the enemy troops who pursued them were destroyed.

Don't let your dead ends get the best of you. The same God who delivered the Israelites stands beside you. The Lord will open an unexpected way, a way you've never thought of before.

You can be part of the miracle. Just stand firm.

wade in the water

Last weekend I attended a concert of Sweet Honey in the Rock, an *a capella* quartet of African-American women who sing gospel, blues, jazz, and African music. The audience was widely diverse, the response enthusiastic. One song in particular reverberated in my soul.

It was the old spiritual, "Wade in the Water"—a song I had heard many times, and even sung in various choirs. But this time it struck me with fresh truth. "You gotta step out in faith," one of the women said as the song began. "You gotta get your feet a little wet; gotta put your foot in the river before the Lord will open the way."

Now, wait a minute. Didn't God push back the waters so that the Israelites could cross over on *dry ground*? Wasn't *that* the pattern of redemption?

No doubt that's what the Israelites thought when they finally came to the River Jordan and were about to cross into Canaan. It was the last barrier to the Promised Land. They had already seen God open the waters of the Red Sea; they knew how it was supposed to work. *Just give the word, Joshua, the way Moses did. Hold out your staff, and the water will part.* And now here was Joshua, that young upstart, changing the rules, telling them that this time the priests carrying the Ark of the Covenant would have to step *into* the

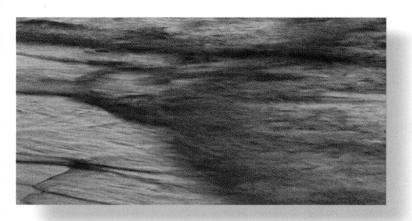

river—at flood stage, no less—before the water would part for them to cross over (Josh. 3:12–13).

That wasn't the way God did it before. This time the miracle happened only when Joshua and the priests were willing to take a risk.

But we don't want to get our feet wet, do we? We don't want to take the chance of stepping into the flood. We might get swept away by the current. We want the Lord to give us the kind of miracle we're accustomed to.

God, however, rarely does things the same way twice. We can't second-guess the Almighty or get pre-approval for our escape route.

When the flood surrounds us, the Lord may part the waters...or enable us to walk on top of them...or provide a boat...or tell us to wade on in.

The method doesn't matter. It's an issue of walking by faith. And faith is the evidence of things *not seen*. We step out, trusting that the dry ground will be there, even if all we see is water.

So go ahead. Wade in the water. Get your feet wet.

And keep your faith-eyes open. You'll see God work in unexpected ways.

fear

In his first Inaugural Address, delivered in March of 1933, President Franklin D. Roosevelt gave the nation a concept that became a rallying cry through years of war, deprivation, and struggle: *"The only thing we have to fear is fear itself..."*

like a

Roosevelt was right—not just about war, but about every aspect of human growth and development. Fear paralyzes. Fear keeps us from moving forward.

flood

But we fear a lot more than fear itself. We fear the unknown, the unanticipated, the unprepared−for conflicts of life. We fear what is within us, and what threatens us from without. We fear downturns in the stock market, layoffs at work, changes in relationships, challenges to our belief systems. Even when things are good, we cling to Murphy's law: *If anything can go wrong, it will.*

But God doesn't want us to live in fear. Fear is the opposite of faith. It wreaks havoc with our ability to trust and undermines the peace that the Lord desires for us.

The Bible presents a marked contrast between those who live in harmony with God and those who don't. "Terrors overtake [the wicked] like a flood," Job says (Job 27:20). But those who "live in the shelter of the Most High...will not fear the terror of the night, or the arrow that flies by day" (Ps. 91:1, 5). It's a comforting concept. But on a practical level, how do we deal with the riptides of fear that threaten to take us under? How do we keep our heads above water when the whirlpool sucks at us and pulls us down?

"Don't fight it," my teacher advised me when I was first learning to swim. "The water will bear you up if you just relax."

Just relax...

It was easier said than done, I'll have to admit. Terrified of drowning, I kept on flailing my arms and legs, trying with all my might to stay on the surface. But then, one day, I just got tired. Tired of struggling. Tired of gulping air and being sure my next breath would be my last. So I gave up.

And with the surrender, I floated to the surface, and the water that had been my enemy became my ally.

When fear overtakes you like a flood, don't let it paralyze you. Relax. Let God's trustworthiness bear you to the surface, to light and air and safety.

Surrender—
not to the fear,
but to your faith.
God
will not
let you
sink.

bitter waters or blessings?

In a recent election, our state held a bond issue for clean water—tax money designated to keep the mountain streams and rivers unpolluted, the environment safe for fish and wildlife, and—ultimately—the drinking water clear. The bond passed, fortunately, but not without a fight. Apparently a lot of people didn't want to spend an extra dollar or two to protect our water sources for the future.

The Israelites in the wilderness faced a "bond issue" of their own. In Exodus 15, they had just come out of Egypt, just witnessed the Pharaoh's troops drowned when the waters of the Red Sea crashed over them. Miriam's song of glory was still ringing in their ears.

Then, three days into the wilderness, they came upon an oasis. But the name of the place was Marah, which means "Bitterness." The waters were undrinkable.

At this point the Israelites had a choice. They could invest a little of their faith and wait to see what God would do on their behalf, or they could give in to the bitterness. They chose the latter. They complained.

Bitterness is a habit that can seriously hinder our spiritual journey. When life becomes difficult, when it doesn't seem as if God is providing for our needs, when we're not getting what we want when we want it, we have a decision to make. We can hold onto our faith and trust that God has an answer in mind, or we can gripe and moan and complain and let our souls become embittered.

The writer of Hebrews warns against bitterness: "See to it that no one fails to obtain the grace of God; that no root of bitterness springs up and causes trouble, and through it many become defiled" (Heb. 12:15).

The verse holds a key for us. When we lose sight of the grace of God, bitterness takes root. But when we keep our eyes fixed on the character of God, on the mercy, grace, and love of the One who liberates us, on the ways our Provider cares for us, we're less likely to become disgruntled when an oasis turns out to be bitter.

At Marah, Moses found that key—the grace that conquers bitterness. God showed him a tree, and when Moses threw a branch into the bitter waters, they became sweet (Exod. 15:25). An image, perhaps, of the cross, of the sacrificial love that sweetens even the bitterest experiences of life.

Expecting an oasis, but finding a bitter stream? Don't lose sight of the grace of God. Look to the cross, where the curse is turned into a blessing.

shipwreck

A few years ago, my parents booked a cruise to Alaska. They flew to Vancouver, boarded the well-appointed ship, and sailed up the coast, looking forward to a week of beautiful scenery and exciting adventure. But the adventure they got wasn't exactly what the cruise line had advertised. On the way in to dock at the first Alaskan port, they heard the sound of impact, felt the deck shudder beneath them. The ship listed to port, and people began to panic. The giant ocean liner had run aground on the rocks.

Shipwreck. The very word evokes images that chill us to the bone. Images of frantic passengers jumping into icy waters. Images of danger, even death. Fortunately, in my parents' case, everyone was evacuated safely and no one was seriously hurt. The situation was more inconvenience than disaster—but still a story my dad elaborates with great drama.

But what about our spiritual life? How can we find a positive story to tell when our faith runs aground, our trust founders, and the waters of life threaten to overwhelm us? This is not just an inconvenience, a vacation abruptly terminated. It's a major disaster, a calamity likely to affect us forever. How do we recover when our faith begins to sink?

We learn from Paul's experience of shipwreck.

In Acts 27–28, Paul set sail for Rome. He was in chains; even so, he knew he was being sent by the Spirit to bring the good news of Jesus Christ to the Romans. Then, as if to thwart God's purposes, a great storm struck. The ship hit a reef and ran aground, and Paul, his companions, and over 200 sailors washed up on Malta, an island unknown to them. Shivering with cold and pelted by winter rains, they began to build a fire. And as if the near–death experience of the shipwreck wasn't enough, a viper came out of the bundle of wood and bit Paul.

Imprisonment. Shipwreck. And just when you think things can't get any worse, a snake in the woodpile. Where is God in all this? What about the promises of protection and provision and abundant life?

Read on. Paul didn't die from the snakebite. The imprisonment, the shipwreck, the viper—all of those adverse experiences gave Paul the opportunity to minister grace and healing to the people of the island. Paul didn't know where Malta was. But God knew.

And God knows where you are, too. Right in the middle of your storm, even if it feels as if you're all alone, hanging onto the wreckage of your faith in the middle of the sea.

Don't let go.

Hold on. The Lord will bring you safely to the shore.

sail on

Catherine and John live on the Kitsap Peninsula, across the Puget Sound from Seattle. Their home fronts on Hood Canal, and John, a retired Navy officer, loves to go sailing and kayaking. Catherine will occasionally join him in the two-person kayak he built, but she's a little nervous about getting into the sailboat unless the wind is calm.

The problem is, calm winds make for very dull sailing, unless you just want to sit on the deck and sun yourself.

In our spiritual lives, too, we don't get anywhere without taking a bit of a risk. We need a bit of wind and a few waves to move us toward our destination.

"Some went down to the sea in ships," the psalmist says. "They saw the deeds of the LORD, his wondrous works in the deep. For he commanded and raised the stormy wind, which lifted up the waves of the sea" (Ps. 107:23–25).

These sailors knew that the wind and waves were necessary to bear them along. But when "they mounted up to heaven" and "went down to the depths, their courage melted away in their calamity."

So it is with us. We want to grow, to change, to be challenged in our faith, but when the challenges become a bit more dangerous than we had counted on, our courage fails us. We cry out for calm waters and still winds. We'd rather get a tan than make progress on the journey.

God, however, doesn't let us have our way. The Lord calls us to stretch our souls, to reach a little further than we have before, to go the distance, to square our sails and tack into the wind.

We don't like it. We fuss and argue and try to go our own way. But when we finally relent, when we come through the test, we discover that we are stronger than we thought we were. We no longer have to base our perceptions of God or ourselves

on what other people have taught us.
We no longer need to hang onto our
preconceived notions of who the Lord is
and what the Spirit might call us to do.
We've done it. We've gone through the
wind and waves and come out changed.

The waters are not always calm,
but God is in control. And when we
trust that truth, we find ourselves
brought to a new place, a place that
strengthens our hearts, nurtures our
souls, and feeds our faith.

So don't panic when the winds
kick up and waves grow strong. Hoist
your sail, prepare for adventure. The
One who created, redeemed, and loves
you is at the helm. Sail on!

part six

Reflections in a Quiet Pool

See, the streams of living waters,
  springing from eternal Love
Well supply thy sons and daughters,
  and all fear of want remove.

—John Newton

in the image of God

According to *People* magazine, he's "the sexiest man alive." He's been Han Solo and Indiana Jones. In real life he's Harrison Ford, star of blockbuster movies like *Star Wars, Regarding Henry, Working Girl,* and *Raiders of the Lost Ark.* One of the most popular, most influential, and probably most wealthy actors in Hollywood.

But what does Harrison Ford think of this new honor? He shrugs and gives a self-effacing laugh. "It's ridiculous." Apparently he's not nearly as concerned with his image as others are.

In the modern world, we think a lot about image. About projecting the right impression to get a better job or a promotion. About presenting ourselves in the best light so that others will like us or respect us— or even fear us. Image, they say, is power.

But for us as Christians, image is more than just wearing clothes designed to hide our flaws, finding the right hair color or the best make-up artist. Image goes to the very core of our being. For we are made in the image of Almighty God.

The story of creation tells us, "God created humankind in his image, in the image of God he created them, male and female..." (Gen. 1:27). What a wonderful legacy! You and I, despite our human weaknesses and frailties, bear in our deepest souls the indelible imprint of God's hand.

It should be—and can be—a truth that shapes our hearts and directs our lives. We are God's people, lovingly fashioned in the likeness of the One who made us and called us to follow. We are on a journey that leads to growth and change. With every step we become increasingly a reflection of the Lord who stamped us with the Divine Image.

But sometimes we forget who we are. We lose sight of where we are going. We focus on the failures of the past instead of the possibilities for the future. We need to be reminded that we do not travel on this journey alone.

Sit for a moment beside the quiet stream. Gaze into a still pool. The reflection you see is not simply the wavering image of a wandering soul. It is the face of one who has been touched by the Creator, set free by the Redeemer, empowered by the Spirit.

It is you, but it is more than you. It is God within you, transforming you, working through you to reach the world with grace.

living with purpose

Our church is in the process of looking for new worship space. We've outgrown our present building; youth and adult Sunday school classes are meeting in an architect's office across the street, and covered-dish dinners have become an exercise in very close fellowship. The Facilities Task Force has spent months doing walk-throughs and surveys to evaluate our options. Do we buy another church? Buy land and build? Add on?

Then, just last week, a representative of the denomination told us that we were going about it all wrong. "First," she said, "you have to be clear about your vision for the future, your *purpose* as a congregation. Is your primary goal worship and teaching, or outreach to the community? The answer to that question will determine not what kind of building you *want*, but what kind of building you *need*."

It's true of us as individual Christians, too. If we truly want to reflect the image of God in our personal lives and our relationships with others, we have to be clear about our purpose. Discovering what God has called us to will shape who we become and what we do with our lives.

But sometimes we get confused about the Lord's calling. We look around for a burning bush telling us to set the captives free; we wait through a long night of prayer expecting to hear the voice of God sending us to be a missionary or to preach the gospel in the inner city.

Yet what we do, as important as it may be, is secondary to our larger purpose for living. And what is that purpose? Romans 8:28–29 tells us: "Those who love God...are called according to his purpose...to be conformed to the image of his Son." This is the higher calling and purpose of God—to be conformed to the likeness of Christ. To allow the Holy Spirit to work in us to purify and clarify the Divine Image that was imprinted upon human life at creation. Whatever we do grows out of that image, a response to the transforming power of God within us.

When we understand that our mission in life is to be like Jesus, that truth will change us forever. The question is not so much "What would Jesus *do*?" but "Who would Jesus *be*?" That is, what is the character of Christ like, and how do we seek to emulate it?

At the most fundamental level, Jesus was a person who lived in communion with God. A person who gave priority to internal matters like forgiveness and love and acceptance and self-awareness. A person who saw the world and everyone around him through spiritual eyes. The things he *did*—feeding the hungry, healing the sick, forgiving sin, defending the disenfranchised, speaking the truth—reflected character traits of love, justice, honesty, peace, and a mind in sync with God.

Jesus knew what mattered. He lived with purpose—and you can, too.

Look first to your purpose for living, and everything else will fall into place.

too busy _doing_ to think of _becoming_

There was a big argument on the _Oprah Winfrey Show_ the other day. Some well-meaning religious folks were taking Oprah to task about the new focus for her show—"Remembering Your Spirit." She was saying, quite simply, that human beings are more than the sum of their physical and intellectual lives, more than what they can acquire or do in this life. There is something else—she called it "spirit"—that guides our lives and motivates our actions. One outspoken woman objected strenuously. "Spirit," she said, refers exclusively to the Holy Spirit, and the Holy Spirit is a force apart from and outside human experience. Oprah could not refer to the essence of human life as "spirit" without being guilty of heresy.

I'll have to confess to siding with Oprah on this one. We human beings _do_ have a spirit—a central core that connects us to truth beyond ourselves.

God's Spirit, Romans 8:16 tells us, "bear[s] witness with our spirit that we are children of God." As humans with free will, we can choose whether or not we will allow our spirits to be empowered by the Spirit of Christ, but whether we do or not, we still have a spirit that governs our lives.

Ironically, a lot of people who would never identify themselves as Christians seem to be more in touch with that inner self than we are. They look deep inside, seeking to understand their hidden motives and secret longings. Many of them find a center of peace and tranquility that sustains them. We may not agree with their motives or their conclusions, but we have to admit that they've found _something_ that brings them joy and strength.

How much more should we, whose spirits are linked to the Spirit of the Almighty, find that inner place of peace? How much more should we be aware of the very marrow of our beings, the key to who we are and how we relate to God and others?

Unfortunately, we don't always take the time or effort to explore the inner self. We're too busy *doing* to think very much about *becoming*.

Still, if we're honest with ourselves, we have to face the truth that *becoming* is important to God. "Let your adornment be the inner self," Peter says, "with the lasting beauty of a gentle and quiet spirit, which is very precious in God's sight" (1 Pet. 3:4).

Do you want the reflection of the Lord to shine from your life? Do you want to see the image of Christ developed more fully within you? Then look to Jesus, who was in touch with that inner self. Jesus, according to John 13:3, knew who he was, where he had come from, and where he was going. And that knowledge enabled him to wash feet, to serve, to live as an example of a gentle and quiet spirit.

Be still. Listen.

Look into your heart.

You will discover who you are—

that adornment of the inner spirit,

which is precious in God's sight.

We like to be thought of as honest people, especially if we're Christians. But the truth is, most of us have lied on occasion. We've told our neighbors their new baby daughter is beautiful, even if she's bald and wrinkled and resembles a little old man. We've told the bride she's stunning, withholding the fact that the dress she's chosen makes her appear fifty pounds heavier. We've let an old friend enjoy his mid-life crisis without informing him that he looks ridiculous heaving himself out of his red Ferrari convertible.

But when it really counts, when the stakes are high and the impact is eternal, we're always completely honest.

poured out like water

Or are we?

Don't we lie to ourselves... to others...even to God? We claim that everything's just fine, even when we're struggling with depression. We mouth "spiritually correct" platitudes about trusting God and knowing that the future is in good hands, even when we're anxious or frustrated, or so angry with the Lord we could scream. As if we believed that God didn't know better.

Reflecting the image of God in our lives, being conformed to the likeness of Christ, includes being honest with ourselves and with the Lord, even if that honesty makes us look less spiritual in the eyes of those around us. Jesus was open with God, after all, when he prayed in the Garden of Gethsemane, "Let this cup pass from me." He was honest when he rebuked the disciples and displayed anger with the moneychangers in the temple. The prophet Jeremiah was candid enough with the Lord to write an entire book of lamentations over the destruction of Jerusalem. He was angry, and he let God know it.

So when Jeremiah writes, "Pour out your heart like water before the presence of the LORD" (Lam. 2:19), it's no theoretical advice. Our hearts cannot be healed and liberated when they're filled with unexpressed bitterness, anger, or despair.

Are you frustrated, confused, mad at God? Go ahead, say it out loud. God already knows what you're feeling. You won't be struck down for your honesty. Being open with the Lord is not just a catharsis, but an expression of trust. It is reaching out in faith to One who listens and loves.

Be honest, with yourself and with the Lord.

Pour out your heart like water.
It can become a cleansing,
healing flood.

t r a n q u i l i t y

It's mid-November. Thanksgiving is exactly ten days away. I have a dozen people coming for Thanksgiving dinner—most of them vegetarian—and haven't even begun to think about what to serve. The house needs cleaning; the guest room hasn't seen a dust rag in over a month. And wasn't it just last week that we had that big Fourth of July party?

Martha, Martha, you are upset about many things...

Make that *obsessed* about many things. Too little time. Too much to do. Hurry, hurry. Worry, worry. It's easy to miss that still, small voice:

"Peace I leave with you; my peace I give to you. I do not give it to you as the world gives. Do not let your hearts be troubled, and do not let them be afraid" (John 14: 27).

Oh, really? Fine for you to say, Jesus—you don't understand the pressures I'm facing. You don't know what it's like, bearing all this responsibility...

And amid all my agitation, I hear that Voice again:

Shhh. Settle yourself. Sit down beside the quiet stream, and listen. Look into the pool, and see my character reflected there.

The image of Christ is a picture of tranquility, not of turmoil. But sometimes it's hard for us to stop and heed the quieting voice of God. Our narrow, limited experience makes us believe—if only for a moment—that the Lord could never understand the obligations and pressures of modern life.

But Jesus does understand. He spent a good part of his earthly ministry with crowds pressing around him, clamoring for bread and healing. In the last days of his life, he was pursued by the authorities, who sought to put him to death. And what did he do? He went away to a quiet place—to the mountains, to the sea, to the Garden. He spent time alone with God. He found refreshing and renewal and strength to go on in the presence of the One who had sent him.

"A tranquil mind," Proverbs 14:30 reminds us, "gives life to the flesh." Tranquility is not so much a condition of circumstance as a state of mind. That's why even in our busy-ness, we can experience peace if we keep our minds focused on the Source and Giver of that peace.

both sides of the picture

I sat in the pew and tried vainly to keep a straight face as the pastor gave the children's sermon. "What does Jesus look like?" he asked. He held a mirror in his hand, and I knew what was coming. He was going to show each child the mirror, and tell a little story about how we don't really know what Jesus looked like, but how Christ should be reflected in all of us.

The deeper point, however, got railroaded by an angelic-looking child with an incisive sense of righteousness. "Of *course* we know what Jesus looks like," she protested in a determined voice. "We've got a picture of him downstairs in the Sunday school room. He's pale and sick-looking, with long hair and a beard and very sad eyes. They told us bad people killed him, but I think he really died of *malatrition*."

It was a hilarious commentary on our image of Jesus—but a pretty accurate one. Many artistic renderings of the Savior *do* make Christ look anorexic, anemic, and profoundly depressed. And sometimes we buy into the image.

Certainly the Bible adds validity to that picture. Jesus the gentle shepherd, the suffering servant, the sacrificial lamb. But there's another side to Jesus, too—a side we need to embrace if we hope to grow in the likeness of Christ and reflect the Divine Image in our own lives. Immanuel, God With Us, is also an agent of justice, a defender of the weak, a strong and mighty advocate.

"The Spirit of the Lord is upon me," Jesus declared, reading from the scroll of Isaiah in the temple, "because he has anointed me to bring good news to the poor. He has sent me to proclaim release to the captives and recovery of sight to the blind, to let the oppressed go free...." Then, with everyone watching, he returned the scroll and said, "Today this scripture has been fulfilled in your hearing" (Luke 4:18–21).

And Jesus' ministry bore out the truth of his declaration. He stood up for the weak, spoke out on behalf of those who had no voice, healed the sick, defended the abused and neglected, protected the afflicted. He gave us an example to follow—an example that came straight from the heart of God.

Do you want to know what Jesus looked like? Consider the scriptural picture of the one we call Savior and Lord. Gentle? Yes. Loving? Certainly. But Jesus was no wimp, no doormat. He was committed unreservedly to justice, righteousness, and truth.

When Christ's reflection shines in us, we will be, too.

It was a bold request, even audacious. But Moses needed a little reassurance. God had instructed him to lead the people from Mount Sinai, where he had received the commandments, toward the Promised Land. And so Moses said, "Show me your ways; show me your glory" (Exod. 33:13, 18).

in the cleft of the rock

What he got was what we all get when we make such a request—a glimpse of the glory, a fleeting glance. "I will make all my goodness pass before you," the Lord responded, "but you cannot see my face; for no one shall see me and live." And so the Lord put Moses into a cleft of the rock. "I will cover you with my hand until I have passed by," God said, "then I will take away my hand, and you shall see my back; but my face shall not be seen" (Exod. 33:19–23).

We long to see the face of God, to be assured of the Lord's presence in our lives. But the glory and the power are too much for us; we cannot behold God's face and live. We can only see reflections, sidelong flashes of the Divine.

So where do we get a glimpse of God? The Psalmist tells us: "I shall behold your face in righteousness; when I awake I shall be satisfied, beholding your likeness" (Ps. 17:15).

We may not look upon the Lord's face directly, but in *righteousness* we get a pretty good picture of God's character. Like Moses standing in the cleft of the rock while God's glory passes by, we are blessed to see the backside of our Creator. We see where the Lord has been; we see the results of the Divine Presence.

And for us, as for Moses, there is a glowing reminder of being in that Presence. When Moses came down from the mountain, he "did not know that the skin of his face shone because he had been talking with God" (Exod. 34:29).

People can tell when we've truly seen God. We don't have to proclaim it or explain it or convince those

around us. It shows. When we've been in presence of the Lord, the likeness of the Almighty will shine within us and out from us, illuminating the darkness and giving off a reflection of holy love and grace.

Do you desire to see the Lord? Do you want that likeness to be reflected in your life? You only need to ask, as Moses did: "Show me your glory. Show me your presence."

But be warned—it's not a particularly safe prayer. The face of God is revealed in righteousness. It's the holiest of close encounters, a transforming experience that will leave you changed...awed...and full of light.

Step into the cleft of the rock. The glory of God is passing by.

a (really) new mind

I recently saw a television commercial that completely baffled me. "You've always trusted Excedrin for headaches," the persuasive voice said. "Now that same great formula is for migraines, too." Two bottles of Excedrin came up on the screen—one plain old Excedrin, and the second with a different label: *New Excedrin for Migraine*.

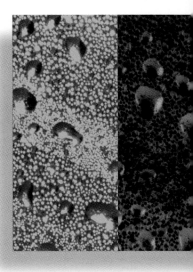

Excuse me? Didn't the guy just say that it was the "same formula"? Then why on earth spend millions of dollars on prime-time advertising just to hawk a repackaged product that hasn't changed in fifteen years? How stupid do they think we are?

Pretty stupid, apparently, because it's a common advertising ploy. Change the flavor, get a new logo, add a fresh scent, and bingo! Sales skyrocket. People will buy anything that's labeled "New."

Sadly, we do it in our Christian lives, too. We latch onto the newest methods of prayer, Bible study, child-rearing, and relationship enlightenment as if we were sliding off the deck of the *Titanic* and that new idea were the only flotation device in sight. We see the need for change, so we turn over a new leaf. We make resolutions. We want to do something now to bring freshness, newness to our walk with God.

The problem is, repackaging and relabeling accomplishes little, except perhaps to make us look more spiritual in the eyes of those around us. We end up changing the outside, while the inside remains untouched.

God has a better plan. "Be renewed in the spirit of your minds," Paul writes to the church at Ephesus. "Clothe yourselves with the new self, created according to the likeness of God in true righteousness and holiness" (Eph. 4:23–24). And to the church at Rome: "Do not be conformed to this world, but be transformed by the renewing of your minds, so that you may discern what is the will of God—what is good and acceptable and perfect" (Rom. 12:2).

We don't get a new mind—as Paul describes it, "the mind of Christ"—by slapping a new logo on an old product. It's a transforming process that happens over time as we immerse ourselves in the presence of the One who created and redeemed us. We don't just wake up one morning to find ourselves spiritually mature, instantly re-created in Christ's image. It happens so gradually that we may not even be aware of it. But those around us will see the difference.

Transformation is God's job, and it will never be accomplished by human effort. Instead of looking for results, focus on the Lord, who is the source and completion of your renewed mind.

It's not just a new package— it's a whole new product.

it's not _what_ you know,
but _who_ you know

We've all heard it—this sage and depressing bit of advice given to artists, actors, writers, anyone dependent upon public opinion for career success: _Listen, kid, making it in this business doesn't have anything to do with talent or genius or what great things you can do. You gotta get in with the right people, develop a network. It's not what you know, it's who you know._

Cynical advice, but not entirely baseless. Success sometimes does depend upon getting the attention of the right people—people in a position to push for that promotion, to market that talent, to get an audition, to make the critics sit up and take notice.

If we turn that advice around and apply it to our spiritual lives, however, it takes on a whole new—and much more positive—meaning. It's not _what_ you do or what you know, but _who_ you know.

As Christians, we often get caught up in the quest for knowledge and the obsession with activity. We study the Bible, investigate various doctrinal perspectives, work hard to get our theological ducks in a row. We can spout Scripture applicable to any situation and have instant access to all the right answers, no matter how difficult the questions. We give ourselves to good works, wear WWJD bracelets, and pride ourselves on our spiritual accomplishments. But underneath, we're tired. Our inner souls languish.

Sure, it's important to know the right stuff. It's important to do the right things. But in God's sight, something else surpasses knowledge—love, and an intimate relationship with Jesus Christ.

"I pray," Paul writes, "that you may have the power to comprehend, with all the saints, what is the breadth and length and height and depth, and to know the love of Christ that surpasses knowledge, so that you may be filled with all the fullness of God" (Eph. 3:18–19).

Spiritual depth is not based on an accumulation of facts, but on a profound connection with the Lord of the Universe. Karl Marx, they say, memorized the entire New Testament. But what good did it do him, if he didn't behold the face of Christ and give his life to a relationship with the Almighty?

Set aside, for a moment, your theological treatises, your doctrinal statements, and your answers. Put away your *to-do* lists, your bulging Day-Timer, and your schedules. Take a deep breath. Gaze into the still pool of God's love and let the healing, renewing waters refresh you. It's worth a little down time to go deeper with the Lord.

After all, it's not *what* you know...it's *who* you know.

from glory to glory

A change is coming; can you feel it?

The Lord is calling—you, me, all of us—to something different, something deeper, something better than we've ever known. A metamorphosis is on its way, a transformation that will make all the difficulties of the journey—the dark nights, the stormy days, the rapids, whirlpools, and riptides of human experience—seem like tiny ripples on the surface of the stream.

The change doesn't come because we work at it, because we grit our teeth and clench our fists and will it into existence. It doesn't happen because we pray for it night and day, study how to get it, or make it happen by the force of our conviction.

It's a gift from the heart of the Creator, a grace bestowed by the One who loves us.

"All of us, with unveiled faces, seeing the glory of the Lord as though reflected in a mirror, are being transformed into the same image from one degree of glory to another; for this comes from the Lord, the Spirit" (2 Cor. 3:18).

Believe it. Accept it by faith. We are being transformed from one degree of glory to another. This is God's promise.

It's not a promise based on our worthiness, our work, our intelligence, or our spiritual insight. It's not a reward for good deeds, a gold star for doing our homework. It comes from the Lord, the Spirit. It's free, part of our inheritance from the One who adopted us into the Divine family.

God knows how hard you've tried. How tired you get, how empty your soul can feel even when your days and nights are crowded with all you do in the name of the Lord. God knows the longings of your spirit, the unfulfilled places of your heart. God knows your needs, even when you don't have a clue.

To you who are weary, the Spirit whispers:

Lay down your burdens. Come. Rest. Look into my face, and behold the image of One who loves you more than you could possibly imagine. One who cares enough to lift you up and give your soul new life.

The change is coming. From glory to glory, the likeness of God is being revealed in you.

> Let the reflection of Christ shine
> like the morning sun on the water...
> and be transformed.

notes